Cooking Light

simple
suppers

Preparing a quick meal

just got easier, thanks to this book. We've selected the best of three of the most popular *Cooking Light* monthly columns—Superfast, Menu Suggestions, and Dinner Tonight—to create 81 menus. *Simple Suppers* features quick and easy main dishes; ideas for sides, salads, and desserts; and a game plan to get each meal on the table in less than 45 minutes.

This special *Southern Living At HOME*® edition features a full page for each dinner menu as well as a photograph of every serving. There is a menu to satisfy any appetite or dining occasion. The facing page offers some ideas to inspire you. We hope you enjoy this collection.

Mary Creel

Cooking Light
simple suppers

EDITOR	Mary Simpson Creel, M.S., R.D.
ART DIRECTOR	Susan Waldrip Dendy
MANAGING EDITOR	Liz Rhoades
TEST KITCHENS DIRECTOR	Vanessa Taylor Johnson
FOOD STYLIST	Kellie Gerber Kelley
ASSISTANT FOOD STYLIST	M. Kathleen Kanen
TEST KITCHENS STAFF	Sam Brannock, Kathryn Conrad, Mary H. Drennen, Jan Jacks Moon, Tiffany Vickers, Mike Wilson
ASSISTANT ART DIRECTOR	Maya Metz Logue
DESIGNERS	Fernande Bondarenko, Brigette Mayer, J. Shay McNamee
SENIOR PHOTOGRAPHERS	Becky Luigart-Stayner, Randy Mayor
SENIOR PHOTO STYLIST	Cindy Barr
PHOTO STYLISTS	Melanie J. Clarke, Jan Gautro
COPY CHIEF	Susan Roberts
COPY EDITOR	Tara Trenary
PRODUCTION EDITORS	Joanne McCrary Brasseal, Hazel R. Eddins
INTERN	Ashley Boyer
EDITOR IN CHIEF	Mary Kay Culpepper
EXECUTIVE EDITOR	Billy R. Sims
MANAGING EDITOR	Maelynn Cheung
SENIOR FOOD EDITOR	Alison Mann Ashton
SENIOR EDITOR	Anamary Pelayo
ASSOCIATE FOOD EDITORS	Timothy Q. Cebula, Ann Taylor Pittman, Joy E. Zacharia, R.D.
ASSISTANT FOOD EDITOR	Kathy C. Kitchens, R.D.
ASSOCIATE EDITOR	Rachel Seligman
ASSISTANT EDITOR	Cindy Hatcher
CONTRIBUTING BEAUTY EDITOR	Lauren McCann
DIGITAL PHOTO STYLIST	Jan A. Smith
STUDIO ASSISTANT	Celine Chenoweth
COPY CHIEF	Maria Parker Hopkins
COPY RESEARCHER	Johannah Paiva
ADMINISTRATIVE COORDINATOR	Carol D. Johnson
OFFICE MANAGER	Rita K. Jackson
EDITORIAL ASSISTANTS	Melissa Hoover, Brandy Rushing
CORRESPONDENCE EDITOR	Michelle Gibson Daniels

COOKINGLIGHT.COM

EDITOR	Jennifer Middleton
ONLINE PRODUCER	Abigail Masters

OXMOOR HOUSE, INC.

EDITOR IN CHIEF	Nancy Fitzpatrick Wyatt
EXECUTIVE EDITOR	Susan Carlisle Payne
ART DIRECTOR	Keith McPherson
MANAGING EDITOR	Allison Long Lowery
EDITOR	Rebecca Brennan
COPY EDITOR	Jacqueline Giovanelli
EDITORIAL ASSISTANT	Amelia Heying
SENIOR DESIGNER	Emily Albright Parrish
DIRECTOR OF PRODUCTION	Laura Lockhart
PRODUCTION MANAGER	Theresa Beste-Farley
PRODUCTION ASSISTANT	Faye Porter Bonner

Southern Living At HOME®

PRESIDENT	John H. McIntosh, Jr.
VICE PRESIDENT AND GENERAL MANAGER	Laura Taylor
DIRECTOR OF MARKETING AND FIELD DEVELOPMENT	Gary Wright
RESEARCH MANAGER	Jon Williams

ON THE COVER: Grilled Steak and Summer Vegetables with Pesto, page 8

Simple Suppertime Solutions

9

When you crave comfort food in a fraction of the time:

◄ Mini Meat Loaves (page 9)
• Chicken Potpies (page 23)
• Twenty-Minute Chili (page 60)

When you're pressed for time, these menus have make-ahead options:
• Chicken Breasts Stuffed with Artichokes, Lemon, and Goat Cheese (page 24)
• Asian Marinated Striped Bass (page 50)
• Onion Bread Pudding (page 81)
• Smoky Bacon and Blue Cheese Chicken Salad Pitas (page 93)

To enjoy world cuisines at home:
90
• Udon-Beef Noodle Bowl (page 55)
• Caribbean Pork and Plantain Hash (page 15)
• Seared Duck Breast with Ginger-Rhubarb Sauce (page 35)
◄ Falafel-Stuffed Pitas (page 90)

Looking for a classic recipe? Try one of our shortcut versions:
• Herbed Chicken Parmesan (page 30)
• Pepper Steak (page 7)
• Turkey Tetrazzini (page 56)

Use roasted chicken from the supermarket to jump-start one of these meals:
• Chicken and Couscous Salad (page 74)
• Creamed Chicken (page 29)
• Chicken and Barley Stew (page 61)

70

For quick, portable lunches:
• Chicken-Penne Salad with Green Beans (page 67)
• Chicken and Couscous Salad (page 74)
• Orzo Salad with Chickpeas, Dill, and Lemon (page 77)

To round out the entrées already in your repertoire, make one of these dishes:
• Spinach and mandarin orange salad (page 42)
• Green beans with almonds (page 56)
• Spicy coleslaw (page 26)
• Garlic smashed potatoes (page 47)
◄ Peppery cheese breadsticks (page 70)
• Caramel-coconut sundaes (page 32)

Glazed Pork,
page 17

Chicken Scallopini,
page 25

Shrimp Tacos,
page 38

Curried Noodles with Tofu,
page 80

Contents

Beef and Pork

Create hearty meals in quick time with these savory menus that are simple and delicious.

Menu

Pepper Steak

....

Asian rice pilaf

Heat 1 teaspoon vegetable oil and 1 teaspoon dark sesame oil in a large nonstick skillet over medium-high heat. Add ¼ cup chopped green onions, 1 teaspoon minced peeled fresh ginger, and 2 minced garlic cloves; sauté 2 minutes. Stir in 4 cups hot cooked long-grain rice and 2 tablespoons low-sodium soy sauce.

....

Green beans with almonds

....

Lemon sorbet

Game Plan

1 While rice cooks:
  - Mince garlic and ginger for main dish and pilaf
  - Slice steak and bell pepper

2 While meat mixture cooks:
  - Sauté onions, ginger, and garlic for pilaf
  - Steam green beans

Quick Tip:
To mince ginger easily, place a small, peeled piece in a garlic press, and squeeze.

Pepper Steak

You can toss in other vegetables, such as sliced onion or water chestnuts, when you add the red bell pepper.

Total time: 35 minutes

Cooking spray

2 tablespoons all-purpose flour

2 tablespoons bottled minced garlic (about 6 cloves)

1 tablespoon minced peeled fresh ginger

¼ teaspoon salt

⅛ teaspoon black pepper

1 pound sirloin steak, trimmed and cut across the grain into ¼-inch-thick strips

1 cup red bell pepper strips

½ cup beef consommé

1 teaspoon low-sodium soy sauce

1 teaspoon dark sesame oil

1. Heat a large nonstick skillet over medium-high heat. Coat pan with cooking spray. Combine flour and next 5 ingredients (through steak), tossing to coat. Add beef mixture to pan; sauté 3 minutes. Add bell pepper and remaining ingredients to pan; cover and cook 7 minutes or until peppers are crisp-tender, stirring occasionally. Yield: 4 servings (serving size: 1 cup).

CALORIES 197 (28% from fat); FAT 6.2g (sat 1.9g, mono 2.5g, poly 0.8g); PROTEIN 26.5g; CARB 7.7g; FIBER 0.9g; CHOL 69mg; IRON 3.7mg; SODIUM 419mg; CALC 22mg

PHOTOGRAPHY: RANDY MAYOR/STYLING: MELANIE J. CLARKE

Menu

SERVES 4

Grilled Steak and Summer Vegetables with Pesto

Garlic-herb French bread

Cut a baguette into (½-inch-thick) slices. Place bread slices on a baking sheet. Coat bread with olive oil–flavored cooking spray; sprinkle with garlic powder and Italian seasoning. Bake at 350° for 5 minutes or until crisp.

Vanilla low-fat ice cream with caramel sauce

Game Plan

1 Prepare grill, and preheat oven.

2 While grill and oven are heating:
- Cut vegetables
- Combine vegetables with marinade

3 While steak and vegetables are grilling:
- Heat bread

4 Chop grilled vegetables.

Quick Tip: Bottled minced garlic is a smart time-saver. For each garlic clove in a recipe, substitute ½ teaspoon bottled minced garlic.

Grilled Steak and Summer Vegetables with Pesto

Grilling the meat and vegetables at the same time gets dinner on the table quickly. Asparagus, portobello mushroom caps, and corn on the cob are also great grilled.

Total time: 25 minutes

- 1 pound lean boneless sirloin steak, trimmed
- ¾ teaspoon salt, divided
- ½ teaspoon black pepper, divided
- ¼ cup red wine vinegar
- 4 small zucchini, halved lengthwise
- 4 small yellow squash, halved lengthwise
- 2 red bell peppers, quartered
- 4 green onions
- 4 garlic cloves, minced
- Cooking spray
- 2 tablespoons commercial pesto
- Oregano sprigs (optional)

1. Prepare grill or broiler.

2. Sprinkle steak with ¼ teaspoon salt and ¼ teaspoon black pepper.

3. Combine ½ teaspoon of salt, ¼ teaspoon of black pepper, vinegar, and next 5 ingredients (through garlic) in a large zip-top plastic bag. Seal and shake to coat.

4. Place steak on grill rack or broiler pan coated with cooking spray; cook 4 minutes on each side or until desired degree of doneness. Let stand 5 minutes; cut steak into ¼-inch slices. Place zucchini and squash on grill rack or broiler pan coated with cooking spray; cook for 4 minutes on each side or until tender. Place bell peppers and onions on grill rack or broiler pan; cook 2 minutes or just until tender.

5. Coarsely chop vegetables; place in a bowl. Add pesto; stir gently. Garnish with oregano, if desired. Yield: 4 servings (serving size: 3 ounces steak and 1 cup vegetable mixture).

CALORIES 380 (30% from fat); FAT 12.8g (sat 4.5g, mono 6.1g, poly 0.7g); PROTEIN 40.7g; CARB 24.1g; FIBER 9.4g; CHOL 103mg; IRON 6mg; SODIUM 583mg; CALC 159mg

Mini Meat Loaves

A tangy mixture of ketchup and Dijon mustard not only flavors the meat loaves but also acts as a glaze that helps them brown nicely as they cook.

Total time: 35 minutes

½ cup ketchup
1½ tablespoons Dijon mustard
1 pound ground sirloin
¾ cup finely chopped onion
¼ cup seasoned breadcrumbs
½ teaspoon salt
½ teaspoon dried oregano
⅛ teaspoon black pepper
1 large egg, lightly beaten
Cooking spray

1. Preheat oven to 400°.
2. Combine the ketchup and mustard, stirring well with a whisk. Reserve 2½ tablespoons ketchup mixture. Combine remaining ketchup mixture, beef, and next 6 ingredients (through egg) in a large bowl, stirring to combine.
3. Divide beef mixture into 4 equal portions. Shape each portion into a 4 x 2½–inch loaf; place loaves on a jelly-roll pan coated with cooking spray.
4. Spread about 2 teaspoons reserved ketchup mixture evenly over each meat loaf. Bake at 400° for 25 minutes or until done. Yield: 4 servings (serving size: 1 meat loaf).

CALORIES 255 (28% from fat); FAT 7.9g (sat 2.8g, mono 3.2g, poly 0.4g); PROTEIN 27.4g; CARB 15.7g; FIBER 0.9g; CHOL 120mg; IRON 2.7mg; SODIUM 944mg; CALC 31mg

Quick Tip: Using seasoned breadcrumbs rather than an unflavored variety reduces the need for extra spices in the ingredient list.

Menu SERVES 4

Mini Meat Loaves

Steak house–style lettuce wedges
Combine 2 tablespoons crumbled blue cheese, 1 tablespoon fat-free buttermilk, 2 tablespoons fat-free sour cream, 1 tablespoon light mayonnaise, ¾ teaspoon white vinegar, and ¼ teaspoon salt, stirring well with a whisk. Cut a small head of iceberg lettuce into 4 wedges; place a wedge on each of 4 plates. Drizzle each wedge with about 1½ tablespoons dressing.

Mashed potatoes

Game Plan

1 While oven heats for meat loaves:
 • Combine ketchup and mustard
 • Chop onion

2 While meat loaves bake:
 • Prepare lettuce wedges
 • Prepare mashed potatoes

Menu

SERVES 4

Smothered Sirloin Steak with Adobo Gravy

Mixed greens and avocado salad

Combine 4 cups torn romaine lettuce, ½ cup sliced peeled avocado, ½ cup sliced cucumber, and ¼ cup thinly sliced red onion in a large bowl. Combine 2 tablespoons honey, 2 tablespoons white balsamic vinegar, 2 teaspoons Dijon mustard, and 2 teaspoons extravirgin olive oil in a small bowl; stir well with a whisk. Drizzle dressing over salad; toss well.

Corn on the cob

Game Plan

1 Prepare and refrigerate salad and dressing separately.

2 Prepare patties.

3 While steak simmers:
- Microwave corn on the cob
- Toss salad

Smothered Sirloin Steak with Adobo Gravy

You'll only need the sauce from the can of chipotles. Freeze the peppers to use later.

Total time: 40 minutes

- 1 pound ground sirloin
- 1 (7-ounce) can chipotle chiles in adobo sauce
- Cooking spray
- 2 cups thinly sliced onion
- ⅓ cup beef consommé
- 1 teaspoon low-sodium soy sauce
- ½ teaspoon cornstarch

1. Divide beef into 4 portions, shaping each into a ½-inch-thick patty.

2. Drain chipotles in a colander over a bowl, reserving ¼ cup adobo sauce. Reserve chiles for another use.

3. Heat a large nonstick skillet over medium-high heat. Coat pan with cooking spray. Add patties and onion; cook patties 5 minutes on each side. Add adobo sauce and beef consommé; bring to a boil. Cover, reduce heat, and simmer 10 minutes. Combine soy sauce and cornstarch, and add to pan. Bring to boil; cook 1 minute or until thick. Yield: 4 servings (serving size: 1 steak and 3 tablespoons sauce).

CALORIES 203 (33% from fat); FAT 7.4g (sat 2.5g, mono 3g, poly 0.6g); PROTEIN 26g; CARB 6.8g; FIBER 1.3g; CHOL 70mg; IRON 2.6mg; SODIUM 294mg; CALC 20mg

Quick Tip: To remove the seed from an avocado, cut it lengthwise all the way around; twist gently to separate halves. Firmly hit seed with the blade of a heavy knife; twist knife gently, and lift out seed. Scoop out the flesh from the peel with a large spoon.

Cumin-Coriander Sirloin Steak

The combination of cumin, coriander, and ground red pepper creates a tasty rub for the beef. Brown sugar aids in a crusty caramelization.

Total time: 21 minutes

  Cooking spray
  1 tablespoon brown sugar
  ½ teaspoon salt
  ½ teaspoon ground cumin
  ½ teaspoon ground coriander seeds
  ¼ teaspoon ground red pepper
  1 pound boneless sirloin steak
      (about 1¼ inches thick),
      trimmed

1. Preheat oven to 450°.

2. Coat an 8-inch cast-iron skillet with cooking spray. Place pan in a 450° oven for 5 minutes.

3. Combine brown sugar and next 4 ingredients (through pepper), and rub evenly over both sides of steak. Place the steak in preheated pan.

4. Bake at 450° for 7 minutes on each side or until desired degree of doneness. Let steak stand 5 minutes. Cut steak diagonally across the grain into thin slices. Yield: 4 servings (serving size: 3 ounces).

CALORIES 198 (39% from fat); FAT 8.6g (sat 3.4g, mono 3.6g, poly 0.3g); PROTEIN 25.1g; CARB 3.7g; FIBER 0.3g; CHOL 76mg; IRON 2.9mg; SODIUM 350mg; CALC 17mg

Quick Tip: Heating the cast-iron skillet results in a flavorful seared crust on the steak without having to first brown the meat on the stovetop.

Menu
SERVES 4

Cumin-Coriander Sirloin Steak

Sweet potato spears
Peel 1½ pounds sweet potato; cut lengthwise into (½-inch) wedges. Combine potato wedges, 1 tablespoon olive oil, ½ teaspoon salt, ¼ teaspoon dried thyme, ¼ teaspoon black pepper, and ⅛ teaspoon ground nutmeg. Arrange in a single layer on a baking sheet coated with cooking spray; place in oven on bottom rack. Bake at 450° for 25 minutes or until tender, turning once.

Collard greens

Game Plan

1 While oven heats:
  • Prepare sweet potatoes
  • Prepare spice rub for steak
  • Trim steak and coat with spice rub

2 While potatoes roast:
  • Preheat cast-iron skillet
  • Place steak in oven during final 14 minutes of potatoes' cooking time
  • Prepare collard greens

Menu

Beef-Broccoli Lo Mein

Egg rolls with spicy-sweet dipping sauce

Bake 6 frozen white-meat chicken egg rolls (such as Pagoda) according to package directions. While egg rolls bake, combine 1 tablespoon minced green onions, 2 table-spoons low-sodium soy sauce, 1 tablespoon rice vinegar, 2 tablespoons duck sauce, and 1 teaspoon sriracha (hot chile sauce, such as Huy Fong). Serve sauce with egg rolls.

Fortune cookies

Game Plan

1 While oven heats:
- Bring water to a boil for pasta
- Prepare ingredients for lo mein and dipping sauce

2 While pasta cooks:
- Bake egg rolls
- Prepare dipping sauce

3 Cook lo mein meat mixture.

Beef-Broccoli Lo Mein

Asian condiments and sauces have such concentrated flavors, a little goes a long way.

Total time: 33 minutes

- 8 ounces uncooked spaghetti
- 1 teaspoon dark sesame oil
- 1 tablespoon peanut oil
- 1 tablespoon minced peeled fresh ginger
- 4 garlic cloves, minced
- 3 cups chopped broccoli
- 1½ cups vertically sliced onion
- 1 (1-pound) flank steak, trimmed and cut across the grain into long, thin strips
- 3 tablespoons low-sodium soy sauce
- 2 tablespoons brown sugar
- 1 tablespoon oyster sauce
- 1 tablespoon chile paste with garlic (such as Sambal oelek)

1. Cook pasta according to package directions, omitting salt and fat; drain. Combine pasta and sesame oil, tossing well to coat.

2. While pasta cooks, heat the peanut oil in a large nonstick skillet over medium-high heat. Add ginger and garlic; sauté 30 seconds. Add broccoli and onion; sauté 3 minutes. Add steak; sauté for 5 minutes or until done. Add pasta mixture, soy sauce, and remaining ingredients; cook 1 minute or until lo mein is thoroughly heated, stirring constantly. Yield: 6 servings (serving size: 1⅓ cups).

CALORIES 327 (26% from fat); FAT 9.3g (sat 3g, mono 3.6g, poly 1.6g); PROTEIN 21.7g; CARB 39.1g; FIBER 2.9g; CHOL 36mg; IRON 3.6mg; SODIUM 382mg; CALC 47mg

Quick Tip: Partially freeze the flank steak to make it easier to cut into long, thin strips that cook quickly.

Stuffed Peppers

Bringing the sauce to a boil before adding it to the dish cuts down on the cook time.

Total time: 45 minutes

- 1 (3½-ounce) bag boil-in-bag long-grain rice
- 4 medium red bell peppers
- ¾ pound ground sirloin
- 1 cup chopped onion
- ½ cup chopped fresh parsley
- 1 teaspoon paprika
- ½ teaspoon salt
- ⅛ teaspoon ground allspice
- 2 cups bottled tomato-and-basil pasta sauce (such as Classico), divided
- ½ cup (2 ounces) grated fresh Parmesan cheese
- ½ cup dry red wine
  Cooking spray

1. Preheat oven to 450°.

2. Cook rice according to package directions, omitting salt and fat.

3. While rice cooks, cut tops off bell peppers; reserve tops. Discard seeds and membranes. Place the peppers, cut sides down, in an 8-inch square baking dish; cover with plastic wrap. Microwave at HIGH 2 minutes or until peppers are crisp-tender. Cool.

4. Heat a large nonstick skillet over medium-high heat. Add beef and next 5 ingredients (through allspice); cook for 4 minutes or until beef is lightly browned, stirring to crumble. Remove from heat. Add cooked rice, ½ cup pasta sauce, and cheese to beef mixture, stirring to combine.

5. While beef cooks, combine 1½ cups pasta sauce and wine in a small saucepan; bring to a boil.

6. Spoon about ¾ cup beef mixture into each pepper. Place peppers in a 2-quart baking dish coated with cooking spray, and add wine mixture to pan. Cover with foil.

7. Bake at 450° for 20 minutes. Uncover; bake an additional 5 minutes or until lightly browned. Serve peppers with sauce. Garnish with the pepper tops. Yield: 4 servings (serving size: 1 stuffed pepper and ⅓ cup sauce).

CALORIES 347 (20% from fat); FAT 7.9g (sat 3.9g, mono 2.6g, poly 0.7g); PROTEIN 26.6g; CARB 39.9g; FIBER 4.6g; CHOL 55mg; IRON 4.1mg; SODIUM 747mg; CALC 284mg

Menu
SERVES 4

Stuffed Peppers

Sautéed cabbage
Heat 1 teaspoon olive oil and 1 teaspoon butter in a large nonstick skillet over medium-high heat. Add ½ cup thinly sliced onion; sauté 3 minutes. Add 4 cups shredded napa (Chinese) cabbage and ½ teaspoon salt; cook 3 minutes or until cabbage is tender, stirring frequently.

Sugar snap peas

Game Plan

1 While rice cooks:
- Cut tops off peppers, and remove seeds and membranes
- Microwave peppers
- Chop onion and parsley for peppers
- Preheat oven

2 While meat mixture cooks:
- Grate cheese for peppers
- Bring wine mixture to a boil

3 While peppers bake:
- Prepare cabbage
- Prepare snap peas

Quick Tip: Cut down on prep time by using a bag of preshredded cabbage or slaw mix for the sautéed cabbage.

Menu

SERVES 4

Pork Medallions with Olive-Caper Sauce

Vermicelli with garlic and herbs
Cook 8 ounces vermicelli according to package directions, omitting salt and fat; drain. Add 2 tablespoons each of chopped fresh parsley, lemon juice, and olive oil; toss well. Add 2 minced garlic cloves and 1 teaspoon each of dried basil, salt, and black pepper.

Steamed green beans

Game Plan

1 While water for pasta comes to a boil:
- Pound pork
- Chop olives and parsley

2 While pasta cooks:
- Cook pork
- Microwave green beans

Quick Tip: Cooking green beans in the microwave retains their color and more nutrients than other cooking methods.

Pork Medallions with Olive-Caper Sauce

Thin pork medallions cook very quickly, so stand at the stove to watch them carefully.

Total time: 30 minutes

- 1   pound pork tenderloin, trimmed
- ½   teaspoon salt
- ½   teaspoon black pepper
- ¼   cup all-purpose flour
- 1   tablespoon olive oil, divided
- ½   cup dry white wine
- ½   cup fat-free, less-sodium chicken broth
- ½   cup coarsely chopped pitted kalamata olives
- 2   tablespoons capers
- 2   tablespoons chopped fresh flat-leaf parsley

1. Cut pork crosswise into 8 pieces. Place each pork piece between 2 sheets of heavy-duty plastic wrap; pound to ¼-inch thickness using a meat mallet or rolling pin. Sprinkle both sides of pork with salt and pepper.

2. Lightly spoon all-purpose flour into a dry measuring cup; level with a knife. Place flour in a shallow bowl. Dredge pork in flour, turning to coat; shake off excess.

3. Heat 1½ teaspoons oil in a medium nonstick skillet over medium-high heat. Add half of pork; cook 2 minutes on each side or until pork is done. Remove pork from pan; keep warm. Repeat procedure with the remaining oil and pork.

4. Add wine and broth to pan, and bring to a boil, scraping pan to loosen browned bits. Stir in olives and capers; cook 4 minutes or until slightly thick. Serve sauce over pork. Sprinkle with fresh parsley. Yield: 4 servings (serving size: 2 pork medallions, 2 tablespoons sauce, and 1½ teaspoons parsley).

CALORIES 212 (34% from fat); FAT 8.1g (sat 1.8g, mono 5.1g, poly 0.9g); PROTEIN 25.5g; CARB 8.1g; FIBER 0.9g; CHOL 74mg; IRON 2.7mg; SODIUM 894mg; CALC 30mg

Caribbean Pork and Plantain Hash

Use semiripe yellow plantains—not green or soft, ripe black ones. The plantains brown better if not stirred too much as they cook.

Total time: 35 minutes

- 1 tablespoon low-sodium soy sauce
- ¾ teaspoon salt, divided
- ¾ teaspoon dried thyme
- ¼ teaspoon ground ginger
- ¼ teaspoon ground red pepper
- ⅛ teaspoon ground allspice
- 1 pound pork tenderloin, trimmed and cut into ½-inch pieces
- 1½ tablespoons vegetable oil, divided
- 1 tablespoon butter
- 1½ cups coarsely chopped onion
- 1 cup chopped green bell pepper
- 2 large yellow plantains, chopped (about 3 cups)
- ½ teaspoon black pepper
- 4 garlic cloves, minced
- 1 teaspoon habanero hot pepper sauce
- 2 tablespoons chopped fresh cilantro

1. Combine soy sauce, ¼ teaspoon salt, thyme, and the next 4 ingredients (through pork); toss well to coat. Heat 1½ teaspoons oil in a large nonstick skillet over medium-high heat. Add pork mixture; sauté 4 minutes or until done. Remove from pan. Add 1 tablespoon oil and butter to pan. Add onion, bell pepper, plantains, ½ teaspoon salt, and black pepper; cook 6 minutes, stirring occasionally. Stir in garlic; sauté 2 minutes or until plantains are tender. Drizzle with hot sauce, and stir well. Sprinkle with cilantro. Yield: 4 servings (serving size: about 1½ cups).

CALORIES 384 (29% from fat); FAT 12.5g (sat 4g, mono 3.8g, poly 3.7g); PROTEIN 26.8g; CARB 44.9g; FIBER 4.7g; CHOL 81mg; IRON 2.8mg; SODIUM 674mg; CALC 38mg

Quick Tip: Look for bottled mango slices in the produce section of the supermarket.

Menu · SERVES 4

Caribbean Pork and Plantain Hash

Tomato and hearts of palm salad
Cut each of 4 plum tomatoes lengthwise into 8 wedges; place in a medium bowl. Drain 1 (14-ounce) can hearts of palm; cut each heart of palm lengthwise into quarters. Cut each heart of palm quarter in half crosswise; add to tomato wedges. Add ½ cup thinly vertically sliced red onion, 1 tablespoon chopped cilantro, 1½ tablespoons fresh lime juice, 1 teaspoon olive oil, ¼ teaspoon salt, and ¼ teaspoon black pepper.

Mango slices drizzled with lime juice

Game Plan

1 While pork cooks:
- Chop onion
- Chop bell pepper and plantains for hash

2 While plantain mixture cooks:
- Mince garlic
- Prepare salad
- Prepare mango

Menu

**Pork Loin Chops with
Cinnamon Apples**

Buttered poppy seed noodles
*Cook 8 ounces wide egg noodles according
to package directions, omitting salt and fat;
drain. Place noodles in a large bowl. Add
2 tablespoons chopped fresh parsley, 1½
tablespoons butter, 2 teaspoons poppy seeds,
¼ teaspoon salt, and ¼ teaspoon pepper;
toss to combine.*

Green peas

Game Plan

1 While water for noodles comes to
a boil:
  - Peel and slice apples
  - Sprinkle pork with sage mixture

2 While noodles cook:
  - Cook pork and apples
  - Prepare peas
  - Chop parsley for noodles

Pork Loin Chops with Cinnamon Apples

Pork and apples are simply meant for each other. Tart Granny Smiths balance the
caramel sweetness of brown sugar. Braeburn apples work well, too.

Total time: 22 minutes

- 1 teaspoon dried rubbed sage
- ½ teaspoon salt
- ¼ teaspoon freshly ground black
     pepper
- 4 (4-ounce) boneless center-cut
     loin pork chops (about ½ inch
     thick)
- ½ teaspoon vegetable oil
  Cooking spray
- 1 teaspoon butter
- 4 cups (½-inch) slices peeled
     Granny Smith apples (about
     4 medium)
- 1 tablespoon brown sugar
- 1 teaspoon fresh lemon juice
- ½ teaspoon ground cinnamon
  Dash of salt

1. Combine dried sage, ½ teaspoon
salt, and black pepper; sprinkle over
the pork. Heat oil in a large nonstick
skillet coated with cooking spray over
medium heat. Add pork; cook 3 minutes on each side or until done. Remove the pork from pan; cover and
keep warm.
2. Melt butter in pan over medium
heat. Add apples and remaining ingredients; cook 5 minutes or until tender,
stirring frequently. Serve apple mixture with pork chops. Yield: 4 servings
(serving size: 1 pork chop and ¾ cup
apple mixture).

CALORIES 251 (30% from fat); FAT 8.3g (sat 3.1g, mono 3.3g, poly
0.9g); PROTEIN 24.1g; CARB 20.2g; FIBER 2.3g; CHOL 67mg; IRON
0.9mg; SODIUM 388mg; CALC 38mg

Quick Tip: Use a vegetable peeler instead of a paring knife to quickly prep the apples.

Glazed Pork

Pork medallions make an attractive presentation fanned across the plate. The tangy balsamic vinegar, orange juice, and brown sugar in the sauce balance the spicy rub.

Total time: 20 minutes

- 1 pound pork tenderloin, trimmed
- 1 tablespoon all-purpose flour
- 2 tablespoons brown sugar, divided
- ½ teaspoon salt
- ½ teaspoon ground cumin
- ¼ teaspoon ground cardamom
- ⅛ teaspoon ground red pepper
- ¼ cup raisins
- ¼ cup orange juice
- 3 tablespoons balsamic vinegar
- 2 tablespoons capers
- 1 tablespoon olive oil

1. Cut pork crosswise into 16 pieces.

2. Combine flour, 1 tablespoon sugar, salt, cumin, cardamom, and red pepper; rub evenly over pork.

3. Combine 1 tablespoon of sugar, raisins, juice, vinegar, and capers, stirring until sugar dissolves.

4. Heat oil in a large nonstick skillet over medium-high heat. Add pork; cook 2 minutes. Turn pork over; cook 1 minute. Add vinegar mixture; cook 1 minute or until sauce thickens and pork is done. Yield: 4 servings (serving size: 4 pork medallions and 2 tablespoons sauce).

CALORIES 234 (25% from fat); FAT 6.5g (sat 1.5g, mono 3.8g, poly 0.6g); PROTEIN 27.9g; CARB 15.5g; FIBER 1g; CHOL 67mg; IRON 2.1mg; SODIUM 482mg; CALC 20mg

Quick Tip: Using a large nonstick skillet enables you to cook all of the pork tenderloin quickly and evenly in one batch.

Menu   SERVES 4

Glazed Pork

Parmesan couscous
Bring 1 (16-ounce) can fat-free, less-sodium chicken broth to a boil in a saucepan; stir in 1 cup couscous. Remove from heat. Cover and let stand 5 minutes. Fluff with a fork. Stir in 2 tablespoons grated Parmesan cheese and 2 tablespoons chopped fresh parsley.

Iceberg wedges with buttermilk dressing

Game Plan

1 Wash and cut iceberg; refrigerate.

2 Prepare ingredients for pork.

3 While broth comes to a boil for couscous:
- Chop parsley for couscous

4 While couscous stands:
- Cook pork

beef and pork

Menu

SERVES 4

Red Chile Pork Tacos with Caramelized Onions

Fruit Salsa

Combine 2 cups sliced banana, ½ cup diced pineapple, ¼ cup chopped cilantro, 1 teaspoon brown sugar, ¼ teaspoon salt, and 2 diced seeded jalapeño peppers in a large bowl; toss gently.

Green salad

Game Plan

1 Prepare pork.

2 While pork cooks:
- Slice onion
- Chop tomato
- Prepare salad

3 While onion cooks:
- Prepare salsa

Red Chile Pork Tacos with Caramelized Onions

Ancho chile powder gives the pork a mild, slightly fruity chile flavor. Most supermarkets now carry it, but if you can't find it, substitute regular chili powder.

Total time: 45 minutes

- 1 tablespoon ancho chile powder
- 1 teaspoon brown sugar
- ½ teaspoon salt
- 1 pound pork tenderloin, trimmed
- Cooking spray
- 1 teaspoon vegetable oil
- 3 cups thinly sliced onion
- 8 hard taco shells
- ½ cup chopped tomato
- 8 teaspoons chopped green onions

1. Preheat oven to 425°.

2. Combine first 3 ingredients, and rub evenly over pork. Place pork on a broiler pan coated with cooking spray. Bake at 425° for 20 minutes or until a thermometer registers 160° (slightly pink). Remove pork from oven; let stand 5 minutes before slicing.

3. While pork cooks, heat oil in a large nonstick skillet coated with cooking spray over medium heat. Add onion; cover and cook 10 minutes or until onion is golden brown, stirring frequently. Uncover and cook for 1 minute, stirring constantly.

4. Fill each taco shell with about 2 ounces pork, 3 tablespoons sautéed onion, 1 tablespoon tomato, and 1 teaspoon green onions. Yield: 4 servings (serving size: 2 tacos).

CALORIES 304 (30% from fat); FAT 10.2g (sat 2.2g, mono 5.4g, poly 1.8g); PROTEIN 26.9g; CARB 25g; FIBER 4.5g; CHOL 74mg; IRON 2.1mg; SODIUM 444mg; CALC 46mg

Quick Tip: Covering the onions helps them caramelize more quickly and requires less oil.

Meatballs and Rice Noodles

An Asian spin on a classic, pork and beef balls are nestled atop spicy noodles.

Total time: 30 minutes

3 tablespoons chopped shallots
2 teaspoons fish sauce
1 teaspoon fresh lime juice
2 garlic cloves, minced
1 bacon slice
6 ounces ground sirloin
6 ounces lean ground pork
Cooking spray
10 ounces rice vermicelli or thin
rice stick noodles
½ cup warm water
6 tablespoons sugar
¼ cup fresh lime juice
1½ tablespoons fish sauce
2 teaspoons chili garlic sauce
(such as Lee Kum Kee)
4 garlic cloves, minced
1 tablespoon chopped fresh
basil
1 tablespoon chopped fresh
cilantro
1 tablespoon chopped fresh
mint

1. Combine first 5 ingredients in a food processor; process until smooth. Add beef and pork; pulse to combine.
2. Divide meat mixture into 12 equal portions, shaping each into a (1-inch) ball. Heat a large nonstick skillet over medium-high heat. Coat pan with cooking spray. Add meatballs; cook 10 minutes or until meatballs are done, browning on all sides.
3. Cook noodles in boiling water 6 minutes; drain. Combine warm water and next 5 ingredients (through 4 garlic cloves), stirring with a whisk until sugar dissolves. Combine fresh basil, cilantro, and mint. Divide noodles evenly among 4 plates; top each serving with 3 meatballs. Drizzle each serving with about ⅓ cup sauce; sprinkle with about 2 teaspoons herb mixture. Yield: 4 servings.

CALORIES 487 (28% from fat); FAT 15.1g (sat 5.6g, mono 6.6g, poly 1.2g); PROTEIN 19.1g; CARB 66.7g; FIBER 2.1g; CHOL 59mg; IRON 1.9mg; SODIUM 905mg; CALC 36mg

Menu
SERVES 4

Meatballs and Rice Noodles

Sweet and spicy cucumbers
Combine 4 cups thinly sliced cucumber, 3 tablespoons red wine vinegar, ¾ teaspoon sugar, ¼ teaspoon salt, and ¼ teaspoon crushed red pepper in a large bowl, tossing gently to coat.

Fresh mango with toasted coconut

Game Plan

1 While water for noodles comes to a boil:
  • Prepare meatballs
  • Prepare cucumbers
  • Peel and slice mango

2 While meatballs cook:
  • Prepare sauce for meatballs and noodles
  • Chop herbs
  • Toast coconut

Quick Tip: You can grind ¾ pound shrimp in place of ground meats; cook shrimp balls 6 minutes.

Poultry

Savor the variety of everyone's favorite dinner choice, from chicken to Cornish hens.

Menu

Chicken Thighs with Roasted Apples

Broccoli rabe with garlic

Heat 1 tablespoon extravirgin olive oil in a skillet over medium heat. Add 2 smashed peeled garlic cloves; cook 30 seconds or until garlic is fragrant. Add 1½ pounds cleaned and trimmed broccoli rabe, tossing to coat. Reduce heat to medium-low. Add ¼ cup water; cover and cook 9 minutes or until tender, stirring occasionally. Toss with 2 teaspoons lemon juice, ¼ teaspoon salt, and ⅛ teaspoon black pepper.

Soft breadsticks

Game Plan

1 While oven heats for chicken:
  • Prepare apple mixture
  • Skin chicken thighs

2 While chicken roasts:
  • Prepare and cook broccoli rabe
  • Warm breadsticks

Quick Tip:
Leaving the skins on the apples adds color and saves a step.

Chicken Thighs with Roasted Apples

The roasted apples create a flavorful chunky sauce for this rustic dish. Gala apples are a good substitute for Braeburn.

Total time: 43 minutes

  5 cups chopped Braeburn apple (about 1½ pounds)
  1 teaspoon chopped fresh sage
  ¼ teaspoon ground cinnamon
  ⅛ teaspoon ground nutmeg
  4 garlic cloves, chopped
  ½ teaspoon salt, divided
     Cooking spray
  8 chicken thighs (about 2½ pounds), skinned
  ¼ teaspoon black pepper
     Chopped parsley (optional)

1. Preheat oven to 475°.

2. Combine first 5 ingredients in a large bowl. Sprinkle ¼ teaspoon salt over apple mixture; toss well to coat. Spread apple mixture on a jelly-roll pan coated with cooking spray.

3. Sprinkle chicken with ¼ teaspoon salt and pepper; arrange on top of apple mixture. Bake at 475° for 25 minutes or until chicken is done and apple is tender. Remove chicken from pan; set aside, and keep warm.

4. Partially mash apple mixture with a potato masher; serve with chicken. Sprinkle with parsley, if desired. Yield: 4 servings (serving size: 2 thighs and about ⅔ cup roasted apples).

CALORIES 257 (20% from fat); FAT 5.7g (sat 1.4g, mono 1.6g, poly 1.4g); PROTEIN 25.9g; CARB 26.6g; FIBER 3.5g; CHOL 107mg; IRON 1.7mg; SODIUM 405mg; CALC 30mg

PHOTOGRAPHY: RANDY MAYOR/STYLING: MELANIE J. CLARKE

Menu

**Orange Ginger–Glazed
Cornish Hens**

Oven-roasted green beans
*Combine 1 pound trimmed green beans,
2 teaspoons olive oil, ½ teaspoon salt, and
⅛ teaspoon black pepper. Arrange in a
single layer on a baking sheet coated with
cooking spray; place in oven on rack below
hens. Bake at 475° for 10 minutes or until
tender, turning once. Remove from oven;
toss with 2 teaspoons fresh lemon juice.*

Long-grain and wild rice blend

Game Plan

1 While oven heats:
  • Prepare glaze
  • Split and skin hens
  • Bring water to a boil for rice

2 While hens roast:
  • Cook rice
  • Trim green beans
  • Place beans in oven during final 10
    minutes of hens' cooking time

Orange Ginger–Glazed Cornish Hens

Line your pan with aluminum foil for easy cleanup. Don't worry if some of the sweet
glaze burns on the foil; it won't burn on the hens.

Total time: 45 minutes

¾ cup fresh orange juice (about
     3 oranges)
2 tablespoons minced peeled fresh
     ginger
1 tablespoon low-sodium soy sauce
2 tablespoons honey
1 tablespoon water
2 teaspoons cornstarch
2 (1½-pound) Cornish hens,
     skinned and halved
Cooking spray
½ teaspoon salt
½ teaspoon ground ginger

1. Preheat oven to 475°.
2. Combine the first 4 ingredients in a
small saucepan; bring to a boil. Combine water and cornstarch, stirring
with a whisk. Add cornstarch mixture
to juice mixture in pan, stirring with a
whisk. Cook 2 minutes or until thick
and glossy, stirring constantly.
3. Place hen halves, meaty sides up, on
a foil-lined jelly-roll pan coated with
cooking spray, and sprinkle hen halves
with salt and ground ginger. Spoon
juice mixture evenly over hen halves.
4. Insert a meat thermometer into the
meaty part of a thigh, making sure not
to touch bone. Bake at 475° for 25
minutes or until thermometer registers
180°. Yield: 4 servings (serving size: 1
hen half).

CALORIES 188 (18% from fat); FAT 3.8g (sat 1g, mono 1.2g, poly
0.9g); PROTEIN 22.5g; CARB 15.6g; FIBER 0.3g; CHOL 99mg; IRON
1mg; SODIUM 487mg; CALC 19mg

Quick Tip: Cooking the hens and green beans in the oven
together saves time and ensures that everything will be ready at once.

Chicken Potpies

Use a bowl or ramekin as a guide for cutting the dough into circles for the top crusts.

Total time: 32 minutes

½ (15-ounce) package refrigerated pie dough (such as Pillsbury)
Cooking spray
⅛ teaspoon salt
2 tablespoons all-purpose flour
1 teaspoon dried rubbed sage
¼ teaspoon salt
¼ teaspoon black pepper
8 ounces chicken breast tenders, cut into bite-sized pieces
1¼ cups water
1½ cups frozen mixed vegetables
1 cup mushrooms, quartered
1 (10½-ounce) can condensed reduced-fat, reduced-sodium cream of chicken soup

1. Preheat oven to 425°.

2. Cut 3 (4-inch) circles out of dough; discard remaining dough. Place circles on a baking sheet coated with cooking spray. Lightly coat dough circles with cooking spray; sprinkle evenly with ⅛ teaspoon salt. Pierce top of dough with a fork. Bake dough circles at 425° for 8 minutes or until golden.

3. Combine flour, sage, ¼ teaspoon salt, and pepper in a zip-top plastic bag; add chicken. Seal bag, and toss to coat. Heat a large nonstick skillet over medium-high heat. Coat pan with cooking spray. Add chicken mixture; cook 5 minutes, browning on all sides. Stir in water, scraping pan to loosen the browned bits. Stir in vegetables, mushrooms, and soup; bring to a boil. Reduce heat, and cook 10 minutes. Spoon 1 cup of chicken mixture into each of 3 (1-cup) ramekins or bowls; top each serving with 1 crust circle. Yield: 3 servings (serving size: 1 pie).

CALORIES 374 (27% from fat); FAT 11.4g (sat 4.8g, mono 4.2g, poly 1.2g); PROTEIN 24.1g; CARB 42.6g; FIBER 4.6g; CHOL 58mg; IRON 1.9mg; SODIUM 882mg; CALC 38mg

Quick Tip: Use two cups of cooked chicken in place of breast tenders.

Menu   SERVES 3

Chicken Potpies

Spinach and orange salad
Combine 5 cups packaged baby spinach, 1 cup drained mandarin oranges in light syrup, and ¼ cup slivered red onion. Combine 2 tablespoons balsamic vinegar, 1 tablespoon honey, 2 teaspoons Dijon mustard, 1 teaspoon olive oil, ⅛ teaspoon salt, and ⅛ teaspoon black pepper, stirring with a whisk. Drizzle vinaigrette over salad; toss gently to coat.

Chocolate low-fat ice cream with graham crackers

Game Plan

1 While oven heats for piecrusts:
• Prepare flour mixture for chicken
• Cut chicken into bite-sized pieces
• Prepare vinaigrette for salad

2 While crusts bake:
• Cook chicken mixture
• Prepare salad
• Place dessert bowls in freezer

Menu

Chicken Breasts Stuffed with Artichokes, Lemon, and Goat Cheese

....

Bulgur pilaf with pine nuts

Heat 2 teaspoons olive oil in a medium skillet over medium-high heat. Add 1 cup coarse bulgur, ⅓ cup sliced green onions, ⅓ cup chopped shiitake mushrooms, and ⅛ teaspoon salt; sauté 5 minutes. Stir in 1 (14-ounce) can fat-free, less-sodium chicken broth; bring to a boil. Cover, reduce heat, and simmer 15 minutes. Remove from heat; let stand, covered, 5 minutes. Stir in 2 tablespoons pine nuts and 2 tablespoons chopped fresh parsley.

....

Wilted spinach

....

Game Plan

1 While bulgur cooks:
  • Combine cheese mixture
  • Pound chicken
  • Stuff chicken

2 While chicken cooks:
  • Prepare spinach
  • Finish pilaf

Chicken Breasts Stuffed with Artichokes, Lemon, and Goat Cheese

Browning the chicken on the stovetop and finishing it in the oven frees you to put the final touches on the pilaf. Wilt the spinach just before the chicken is done.

Total time: 43 minutes

2½	tablespoons Italian-seasoned breadcrumbs
2	teaspoons grated lemon rind
¼	teaspoon salt
⅛	teaspoon black pepper
1	(6-ounce) jar marinated artichoke hearts, drained and chopped
1	(3-ounce) package herbed goat cheese, softened
4	(6-ounce) skinless, boneless chicken breast halves

Cooking spray

1. Preheat oven to 375°.

2. Combine the first 6 ingredients in a medium bowl; stir well.

3. Place each chicken breast half between 2 sheets of heavy-duty plastic wrap; pound to ¼-inch thickness using a meat mallet or rolling pin. Top each breast half with 2 tablespoons cheese mixture; roll up jelly-roll fashion. Tuck in sides, and secure each roll with wooden picks.

4. Heat a large nonstick skillet over medium-high heat. Coat pan with cooking spray. Add chicken to pan; cook 3 minutes on each side or until browned. Wrap handle of pan with foil; bake at 375° for 15 minutes or until chicken is done. Yield: 4 servings.

CALORIES 234 (30% from fat); FAT 7.8g (sat 3.5g, mono 1.4g, poly 0.5g); PROTEIN 33g; CARB 7.2g; FIBER 1.5g; CHOL 78mg; IRON 1.6mg; SODIUM 545mg; CALC 49mg

Quick Tip: You can prepare the artichoke-cheese filling, stuff the chicken breasts, and chill up to four hours before serving.

Chicken Scallopini

Pounding the chicken breast halves into thin "scallops" cuts the cooking time in half but leaves the chicken moist and tender. Add a sprig of fresh flat-leaf parsley for a garnish.

Total time: 22 minutes

- 4 (6-ounce) skinless, boneless chicken breast halves
- 2 teaspoons fresh lemon juice
- ¼ teaspoon salt
- ¼ teaspoon black pepper
- ⅓ cup Italian-seasoned breadcrumbs
- Cooking spray
- ½ cup fat-free, less-sodium chicken broth
- ¼ cup dry white wine
- 4 teaspoons capers
- 1 tablespoon butter

1. Place each chicken breast half between 2 sheets of heavy-duty plastic wrap; pound to ¼-inch thickness using a meat mallet or rolling pin. Brush chicken with juice; sprinkle with salt and pepper. Dredge chicken in the breadcrumbs.

2. Heat a large nonstick skillet over medium-high heat. Coat pan with cooking spray. Add chicken to pan; cook 3 minutes on each side or until chicken is done. Remove from pan; keep warm.

3. Add broth and wine to pan; cook 30 seconds, stirring constantly. Remove from heat. Stir in capers and butter. Yield: 4 servings (serving size: 1 chicken breast half and 1 tablespoon sauce).

CALORIES 206 (20% from fat); FAT 4.6g (sat 2.2g, mono 1.3g, poly 0.5g); PROTEIN 29.2g; CARB 7.7g; FIBER 0.6g; CHOL 76mg; IRON 1.6mg; SODIUM 657mg; CALC 27mg

Quick Tip: Use two teaspoons bottled minced garlic instead of two fresh cloves for the side dish.

Menu
SERVES 4

Chicken Scallopini

Orzo, tomato, and zucchini toss
Heat 1 teaspoon olive oil in a medium skillet over medium-high heat. Add 1 cup halved cherry tomatoes, 1 cup chopped zucchini, and 2 minced garlic cloves; sauté 2 minutes. Stir in ½ teaspoon Italian seasoning and ¼ teaspoon red pepper flakes; sauté 1 minute or until zucchini is crisp-tender. Combine tomato mixture, 3 cups hot cooked orzo, and ¼ teaspoon salt; toss well.

Garlic bread

Game Plan

1 While orzo cooks:
- Pound chicken
- Season and dredge chicken in breadcrumbs
- Chop tomatoes and zucchini

2 Heat garlic bread.

3 While chicken cooks:
- Prepare tomato mixture for orzo, tomato, and zucchini toss

Menu

**Chicken Soft Tacos with
Sautéed Onions and Apples**

Spicy coleslaw

*Combine 4 cups shredded cabbage, ⅓ cup
thinly sliced red onion, ¼ cup chopped
cilantro, 2 tablespoons fresh lime juice, 2
tablespoons apple cider vinegar, ½ teaspoon
salt, ¼ teaspoon ground red pepper, and
¼ teaspoon brown sugar, tossing well.*

Canned refried beans

Game Plan

1 While pan preheats:
  • Cut chicken into bite-sized pieces

2 While onion mixture cooks:
  • Warm refried beans

3 Prepare coleslaw.

4 Warm tortillas.

Chicken Soft Tacos with Sautéed Onions and Apples

In this recipe, a savory-sweet taco filling is encased in warm flour tortillas.

Total time: 35 minutes

- 1 tablespoon olive oil
- 1 pound skinless, boneless chicken breast, cut into bite-sized pieces
- ½ teaspoon salt
- ½ teaspoon ground nutmeg
- ½ teaspoon freshly ground black pepper
- 1 tablespoon butter
- 2 cups thinly sliced onion
- 2 cups thinly sliced peeled Granny Smith apple (about 2 apples)
- 2 garlic cloves, minced
- 8 (6-inch) flour tortillas

1. Heat oil in a large nonstick skillet over medium-high heat. Sprinkle the chicken evenly with salt, nutmeg, and pepper. Add chicken to pan; sauté for 7 minutes or until golden. Remove chicken from pan; keep warm.

2. Melt butter in pan over medium heat. Add onion; cook 4 minutes or until tender, stirring frequently. Add apple; cook 6 minutes or until golden, stirring frequently. Add garlic; cook 30 seconds, stirring constantly. Return chicken to pan; cook 2 minutes or until thoroughly heated, stirring frequently.

3. Heat tortillas according to package directions. Arrange ½ cup of chicken mixture evenly over each tortilla. Yield: 4 servings (serving size: 2 tacos).

CALORIES 454 (25% from fat); FAT 12.6g (sat 3.8g, mono 6.1g, poly 1.5g); PROTEIN 32.9g; CARB 51.5g; FIBER 4.8g; CHOL 73mg; IRON 3.3mg; SODIUM 705mg; CALC 116mg

Quick Tip: Bagged shredded cabbage will save a preparation step.

Lemony Spanish Pepper Chicken

While the chicken simmers, you can roast the green beans and cook the egg noodles.

Total time: 45 minutes

8 chicken thighs (about 2½ pounds), skinned
1½ teaspoons dried oregano
½ teaspoon salt
¼ teaspoon black pepper
¼ teaspoon paprika
Cooking spray
1½ cups red bell pepper strips
1½ cups green bell pepper strips
1 tablespoon grated lemon rind
¼ cup fresh lemon juice
½ cup fat-free, less-sodium chicken broth
2 tablespoons ketchup

1. Sprinkle chicken with oregano, salt, black pepper, and paprika. Heat a large nonstick skillet over medium-high heat. Coat pan with cooking spray. Add chicken; sauté 3 minutes or until lightly browned. Turn chicken over; top with bell peppers, rind, and juice. Cover, reduce heat, and simmer 30 minutes or until chicken is done. Remove chicken from pan. Combine broth and ketchup in a small bowl. Stir ketchup mixture into pan; bring to a boil. Serve pepper mixture with the chicken. Yield: 4 servings (serving size: 2 chicken thighs and ½ cup bell pepper mixture).

CALORIES 267 (26% from fat); FAT 7.8g (sat 2g, mono 2.4g, poly 2g); PROTEIN 39.4g; CARB 8.7g; FIBER 1.9g; CHOL 161mg; IRON 2.8mg; SODIUM 609mg; CALC 40mg

Quick Tip: Look for skinned, bone-in chicken thighs at the grocery store.

Menu

SERVES 4

Lemony Spanish Pepper Chicken

....

Garlic-pepper green beans

Combine 1¼ pounds trimmed green beans, 2 teaspoons olive oil, ½ teaspoon salt, ¼ teaspoon garlic powder, and ¼ teaspoon black pepper in a jelly-roll pan. Bake at 450° for 10 minutes or until beans are tender and lightly browned, stirring occasionally.

....

Egg noodles tossed with parsley

....

Game Plan

1 While water comes to a boil for noodles:
  • Skin chicken
  • Cut bell peppers
  • Grate lemon rind

2 Cook chicken.

3 While chicken mixture simmers:
  • Prepare and roast beans
  • Cook noodles
  • Chop parsley

Menu

Grilled Chicken Tostadas

....

Brown rice

....

Pineapple refresher

Combine 3 cups pineapple chunks, 1 cup water, and 6 mint leaves in a blender; process until smooth. Transfer pineapple mixture to a pitcher. Add 2 cups cold water, stirring to combine. Serve over ice.

....

Game Plan

1 While rice cooks:
- Season chicken
- Combine slaw and green salsa
- Combine tomato and olives
- Toast pumpkinseed kernels

2 While chicken cooks:
- Prepare pineapple refresher

Quick Tip: Look for fresh pineapple chunks in the refrigerated section of the produce department, or use canned pineapple chunks packed in juice. If you use canned, drain the juice before blending.

Grilled Chicken Tostadas

Fried tortillas usually form the shells for tostadas; grilling lowers the fat. Bottled salsa, canned beans, and preshredded coleslaw make this recipe a snap to prepare.

Total time: 35 minutes

- 4 (6-ounce) skinless, boneless chicken breast halves
- 1 tablespoon fresh lime juice
- 1 tablespoon 40% less-sodium taco seasoning (such as Old El Paso)
- ½ teaspoon sugar
- Cooking spray
- 6 (8-inch) flour tortillas
- 6 cups packaged coleslaw
- 1 (7-ounce) can green salsa
- 4 cups chopped tomato
- ¼ cup sliced ripe olives, chopped
- 1¼ cups fat-free refried beans
- ½ cup (2 ounces) crumbled feta cheese
- 6 tablespoons reduced-fat sour cream
- ¼ cup fresh cilantro leaves
- ¼ cup unsalted pumpkinseed kernels, toasted (optional)

1. Prepare grill or broiler.

2. Brush chicken with juice; sprinkle with seasoning and sugar. Place the chicken on grill rack or broiler pan coated with cooking spray; grill 4 minutes on each side or until chicken is done. Cool slightly. Cut chicken into ¼-inch strips; set aside. Place tortillas on grill rack or broiler pan coated with cooking spray; grill 30 seconds on each side or until tortillas are golden brown.

3. Combine coleslaw and salsa in a medium bowl; toss to coat. Combine tomato and olives; toss gently.

4. Spread about 3 tablespoons beans over each tortilla, and divide chicken evenly among tortillas. Top each serving with about ⅔ cup slaw mixture, ⅔ cup tomato mixture, 4 teaspoons feta cheese, 1 tablespoon sour cream, and 2 teaspoons cilantro. Sprinkle each serving with 2 teaspoons pumpkinseeds, if desired. Yield: 6 servings (serving size: 1 tostada).

CALORIES 361 (23% from fat); FAT 9.2g (sat 3.6g, mono 1.5g, poly 1.2g); PROTEIN 28.7g; CARB 43g; FIBER 6.8g; CHOL 65mg; IRON 3.7mg; SODIUM 844mg; CALC 221mg

Creamed Chicken

This recipe comes together in a flash. Using whole milk gives the dish a creamy, rich flavor that reduced-fat milk can't, and the peas add a touch of color. Serve over rice.

Total time: 25 minutes

½   cup all-purpose flour
2¼ cups whole milk, divided
1   cup frozen green peas, thawed
2   teaspoons chopped fresh sage
1   teaspoon butter
1   (10-ounce) package roasted skinless, boneless chicken breast (such as Perdue Short Cuts), chopped
1   tablespoon fresh lemon juice
¼   teaspoon freshly ground black pepper
Fresh sage sprigs (optional)

1. Lightly spoon flour into a dry measuring cup; level with a knife. Combine flour and ½ cup of milk in a large saucepan over medium heat, stirring with a whisk until mixture is smooth. Stir in 1¾ cups milk. Cook 4 minutes or until mixture is thick, stirring constantly with a whisk.

2. Add peas, chopped fresh sage, butter, and chicken, stirring to combine. Cook 2 minutes or until thoroughly heated. Remove from heat; stir in juice and pepper. Garnish with sage sprigs, if desired. Yield: 4 servings (serving size: about ¾ cup).

CALORIES 232 (23% from fat); FAT 6g (sat 3.6g, mono 1.8g, poly 0.4g); PROTEIN 20.9g; CARB 25.4g; FIBER 2.1g; CHOL 53mg; IRON 2.2mg; SODIUM 1,001mg; CALC 164mg

Quick Tip: If you can't find roasted skinless, boneless chicken, buy a whole roasted chicken, and substitute 2¼ cups chopped cooked breast meat. Add the leftover chicken to soup, pasta, or a salad later in the week.

Menu

SERVES 4

Creamed Chicken

Broiled tomatoes
Combine 2 tablespoons seasoned breadcrumbs, 1 tablespoon grated Parmesan cheese, ¼ teaspoon salt, and ¼ teaspoon freshly ground black pepper, stirring to combine. Add 1½ teaspoons water and ½ teaspoon olive oil, stirring until moist. Halve 4 plum tomatoes lengthwise; sprinkle evenly with breadcrumb mixture. Place tomato halves, cut sides up, in a baking pan coated with cooking spray. Broil 2 minutes or until golden brown.

Hot cooked rice

Game Plan

1 While water for rice comes to a boil and broiler heats for tomatoes:
  • Chop chicken
  • Prepare topping for tomatoes

2 While rice cooks:
  • Prepare chicken
  • Broil tomatoes

Menu

SERVES 4

Herbed Chicken Parmesan

Roasted lemon-garlic broccoli
Combine 6 cups broccoli florets, 1 teaspoon grated lemon rind, 2 teaspoons olive oil, ¼ teaspoon salt, ⅛ teaspoon black pepper, and 2 thinly sliced garlic cloves on a jelly-roll pan coated with cooking spray. Bake at 425° for 15 minutes or until crisp-tender and lightly browned, stirring occasionally.

Hot cooked orzo

Game Plan

1 While oven heats for broccoli and water for orzo comes to a boil:
- Prepare broccoli mixture
- Combine breadcrumb mixture
- Grate provolone cheese

2 While broccoli bakes:
- Cook chicken
- Cook orzo
- Heat pasta sauce

Quick Tip: Look for bagged washed broccoli florets near the packaged lettuces in the produce department.

Herbed Chicken Parmesan

We recommend rice-shaped orzo pasta with this saucy entrée, but you can serve spaghetti or angel hair pasta instead. If you're making the entire menu, roast the broccoli first. When it's done, turn the oven to broil to melt the cheese for this dish.

Total time: 28 minutes

- ⅓ cup (1½ ounces) grated fresh Parmesan cheese, divided
- ¼ cup dry breadcrumbs
- 1 tablespoon minced fresh parsley
- ½ teaspoon dried basil
- ¼ teaspoon salt, divided
- 1 large egg white, lightly beaten
- 1 pound chicken breast tenders
- 1 tablespoon butter
- 1½ cups bottled fat-free tomato-basil pasta sauce (such as Muir Glen Organic)
- 2 teaspoons balsamic vinegar
- ¼ teaspoon black pepper
- ⅓ cup (1½ ounces) shredded sharp provolone cheese

1. Preheat broiler.

2. Combine 2 tablespoons Parmesan, breadcrumbs, parsley, basil, and ⅛ teaspoon salt in a shallow dish. Place egg white in a shallow dish. Dip each chicken tender in egg white; dredge in the breadcrumb mixture. Melt butter in a large nonstick skillet over medium-high heat. Add chicken; cook 3 minutes on each side or until done.

3. Combine ⅛ teaspoon salt, pasta sauce, vinegar, and black pepper in a microwave-safe bowl. Cover with plastic wrap; vent. Microwave at HIGH 2 minutes or until thoroughly heated. Pour sauce over chicken in pan. Sprinkle evenly with remaining Parmesan and provolone cheese. Wrap handle of pan with foil; broil 2 minutes or until cheese melts. Yield: 4 servings.

CALORIES 308 (30% from fat); FAT 10.4g (sat 5.7g, mono 3g, poly 0.6g); PROTEIN 35.9g; CARB 16.2g; FIBER 1.8g; CHOL 88mg; IRON 2.3mg; SODIUM 808mg; CALC 249mg

Chicken Paprikash–Topped Potatoes

The traditional Hungarian dish of chicken and onion in creamy paprika sauce makes a hearty topping for baked potatoes. Dark meat chicken complements the bold flavors.

Total time: 30 minutes

- 4 baking potatoes (about 1½ pounds)
- 4 skinless, boneless chicken thighs (about 12 ounces), cut into bite-sized pieces
- 2 tablespoons all-purpose flour
- 2 teaspoons paprika
- ¾ teaspoon salt
- ¼ teaspoon ground red pepper
- 1 tablespoon butter
- ½ cup coarsely chopped onion
- 1 (8-ounce) package presliced mushrooms
- 2 garlic cloves, minced
- ½ cup fat-free, less-sodium chicken broth
- ¼ cup reduced-fat sour cream
- 2 tablespoons chopped fresh parsley

1. Pierce the potatoes with a fork, and arrange in a circle on paper towels in microwave oven. Microwave at HIGH 16 minutes or until done, rearranging potatoes after 8 minutes. Wrap each potato in foil; let stand 5 minutes.

2. Combine chicken, flour, paprika, salt, and pepper in a large zip-top plastic bag; seal and shake to coat.

3. Melt the butter in a large nonstick skillet over medium-high heat. Add chicken mixture, onion, mushrooms, and garlic; sauté 5 minutes. Add broth; bring to a boil. Cook 6 minutes or until chicken is done and sauce thickens, stirring frequently. Remove from heat; stir in sour cream.

4. Remove foil from potatoes, and split open with fork. Fluff pulp. Divide chicken mixture evenly over potatoes; sprinkle with parsley. Yield: 4 servings (serving size: 1 potato, ½ cup chicken mixture, and 1½ teaspoons parsley).

CALORIES 311 (25% from fat); FAT 8.6g (sat 3.9g, mono 1.9g, poly 1.2g); PROTEIN 22.9g; CARB 36.3g; FIBER 3.4g; CHOL 86mg; IRON 2.6g; SODIUM 619mg; CALC 56mg

Menu — SERVES 4

Chicken Paprikash–Topped Potatoes

Roasted Brussels sprouts
Combine 4 cups trimmed and halved Brussels sprouts, 2 teaspoons melted butter, ½ teaspoon salt, and ¼ teaspoon black pepper on a jelly-roll pan coated with cooking spray. Bake at 425° for 25 minutes or until crisp-tender.

Garlic breadsticks

Game Plan

1 Preheat oven for Brussels sprouts.

2 While Brussels sprouts roast:
- Microwave potatoes
- Prepare chicken mixture for potatoes

Quick Tip: To chop parsley easily, place sprigs in a measuring cup. Use kitchen shears to snip.

Menu

SERVES 4

Tarragon Chicken-in-a-Pot Pies

Green salad

Caramel-coconut sundaes
Sprinkle ¼ cup flaked sweetened coconut on a jelly-roll pan. Bake at 325° for 10 minutes or until golden brown, stirring occasionally. Scoop ½ cup vanilla low-fat ice cream into each of 4 dessert bowls; top each serving with 1 tablespoon fat-free caramel sundae syrup and about 1 tablespoon toasted coconut.

Game Plan

1 Preheat oven for coconut.

2 While coconut bakes:
• Chop onion
• Slice carrot and zucchini
• Cut up chicken

3 While chicken mixture cooks:
• Hollow out bread
• Prepare salad
• Place dessert bowls in freezer

Tarragon Chicken-in-a-Pot Pies

Popular in French cooking, tarragon adds anise flavor to the creamy chicken mixture. Hollowed-out rolls serve as edible, individual bowls that soak up the sauce.

Total time: 36 minutes

    2   tablespoons all-purpose flour
    1   cup 1% low-fat milk
    ½   cup fat-free, less-sodium chicken broth
    ½   cup dry white wine
    1   tablespoon olive oil
    ⅔   cup chopped sweet onion
    1   pound skinless, boneless chicken breast, cut into bite-sized pieces
    1   cup sliced carrot
    1   cup (⅛-inch-thick) slices zucchini
    ½   teaspoon salt
    ½   teaspoon dried tarragon
    ½   teaspoon black pepper
    4   (4.5-ounce) country or peasant rolls

1. Place flour in a small bowl; slowly add milk, stirring with a whisk to form a slurry. Add broth and white wine.

2. Heat oil in a large saucepan over medium-high heat; add onion and chicken. Sauté 2 minutes; stir in carrot and next 4 ingredients (through pepper). Cover, reduce heat, and cook 4 minutes. Stir slurry into chicken mixture; bring to a boil. Cover, reduce heat, and simmer 10 minutes or until thick, stirring occasionally.

3. Cut rolls horizontally 1 inch from tops. Hollow out bottoms of rolls, leaving ¼-inch-thick shells; reserve torn bread and bread tops for another use. Spoon 1¼ cups chicken mixture into each bread shell. Yield: 4 servings.

CALORIES 413 (17% from fat); FAT 7.8g (sat 2.7g, mono 3g, poly 0.7g); PROTEIN 35.7g; CARB 48.8g; FIBER 3.5g; CHOL 68mg; IRON 4.2mg; SODIUM 865mg; CALC 199mg

Quick Tip: Make breadcrumbs for future use with the bread you remove from the rolls. Place the scraps in a food processor, and pulse five to 10 times. Freeze the breadcrumbs in a zip-top plastic bag for up to six months.

Greek Chicken with Capers, Raisins, and Feta

For an even faster dish, use packaged crumbled feta cheese.

Total time: 30 minutes

4 (4-ounce) skinless, boneless chicken breast halves
2 tablespoons all-purpose flour
1 teaspoon dried oregano
1 tablespoon olive oil
1 cup thinly sliced onion
1½ cups fat-free, less-sodium chicken broth
⅓ cup golden raisins
2 tablespoons lemon juice
2 tablespoons capers
¼ cup (1 ounce) crumbled feta cheese
4 thin lemon slices (optional)

1. Place each chicken breast half between 2 sheets of plastic wrap; flatten to ¼-inch thickness using a meat mallet or rolling pin. Combine flour and dried oregano in a shallow dish, and dredge chicken in flour mixture.

2. Heat oil in a large nonstick skillet over medium-high heat. Add chicken; cook 4 minutes on each side. Remove chicken from pan; keep warm. Add onion to pan; sauté 2 minutes. Stir in broth, raisins, and lemon juice; cook 3 minutes, scraping the pan to loosen browned bits. Return chicken to pan. Cover, reduce heat, and simmer for 8 minutes or until chicken is done.

3. Place a chicken breast on each of 4 serving plates. Add capers to sauce in pan. Spoon ⅓ cup sauce over each serving; top with 1 tablespoon cheese. Garnish with lemon slices, if desired. Yield: 4 servings.

CALORIES 256 (23% from fat); FAT 6.5g (sat 1.9g, mono 3.2g, poly 0.7g); PROTEIN 30g; CARB 19g; FIBER 1.3g; CHOL 72mg; IRON 1.6mg; SODIUM 671mg; CALC 71mg

Quick Tip: To steam zucchini, arrange three cups zucchini in a shallow dish; drizzle with water. Cover and vent; microwave at HIGH until crisp-tender.

Menu   SERVES 4

Greek Chicken with Capers, Raisins, and Feta

Curried couscous
Place ⅓ cup water, 2 teaspoons butter, and 1 (14-ounce) can fat-free, less-sodium chicken broth in a medium saucepan; bring to a boil. Stir in ½ teaspoon curry powder, ¼ teaspoon ground allspice, and 1 (10-ounce) package couscous; remove from heat. Cover and let stand 5 minutes. Fluff couscous with a fork.

Steamed sliced zucchini

Game Plan

1 Pound chicken.

2 Brown chicken.

3 Bring broth mixture to a boil for couscous.

4 While the chicken simmers:
• Steam zucchini
• Cook couscous

Menu

SERVES 4

Joe's Special

Crisp oven potatoes

Combine 2¼ cups frozen hash brown potatoes with onions and peppers (such as Ore-Ida Potatoes O'Brien), 1 tablespoon vegetable oil, 1 teaspoon bottled minced garlic, ½ teaspoon salt, ¼ teaspoon hot paprika, and ¼ teaspoon black pepper on a jelly-roll pan coated with cooking spray. Bake at 450° for 20 minutes or until browned, stirring once.

Beer

Game Plan

1 While oven heats for potatoes:
- Combine potato mixture
- Chop onion
- Chop chard

2 While potatoes bake:
- Prepare scramble
- Toast bread

Joe's Special

This San Francisco specialty turns straightforward scrambled eggs into a distinctive dinner. To stay true to the recipe's roots, serve with toasted sourdough bread.

Total time: 30 minutes

- ½ teaspoon dried basil
- ¼ teaspoon salt
- 4 large egg whites
- 3 large eggs
- 4 ounces hot turkey Italian sausage
- 2 cups chopped onion
- 6 cups chopped Swiss chard
- 4 (1½-ounce) slices sourdough bread, toasted

1. Combine first 4 ingredients in a medium bowl, stirring with a whisk.

2. Remove casings from sausage. Cook the sausage in a large nonstick skillet over medium-high heat until lightly browned; stir to crumble. Add onion; cook 3 minutes or until onion is tender. Stir in chard; cover and cook 3 minutes or until chard wilts, stirring occasionally. Uncover and cook 1 minute or until liquid evaporates. Stir in egg mixture; cook 3 minutes or until eggs are set, stirring frequently. Serve with toast. Yield: 4 servings (serving size: 1 cup egg mixture and 1 toast slice).

CALORIES 335 (23% from fat); FAT 8.6g (sat 2.4g, mono 3.3g, poly 1.8g); PROTEIN 20.9g; CARB 43.2g; FIBER 4.3g; CHOL 183mg; IRON 3.7mg; SODIUM 931mg; CALC 116mg

Quick Tip: Replace the chard with packaged, washed spinach. Use baby spinach to avoid chopping altogether.

Seared Duck Breast with Ginger-Rhubarb Sauce

The sweet, spicy heat from the ginger preserves is balanced by tart rhubarb and wine. Chicken breasts can be substituted for duck, if desired.

Total time: 40 minutes

- 2 cups dry red wine
- 1 cup finely chopped rhubarb
- 2 tablespoons finely chopped shallots
- 1 bay leaf
- 1 star anise
- ½ cup ginger preserves
- ½ teaspoon kosher salt, divided
- 2 (12-ounce) packages boneless whole duck breast, thawed, skinned, and cut in half
- ½ teaspoon freshly ground black pepper
- 2 teaspoons olive oil

1. Combine the first 5 ingredients in a large saucepan; bring to a boil. Cook until reduced to 1 cup (about 18 minutes). Stir in preserves and ¼ teaspoon salt; cook 1 minute. Strain wine mixture through a sieve over a bowl; discard solids.

2. Sprinkle duck with ¼ teaspoon salt and pepper. Heat oil in a large nonstick skillet over medium heat. Add duck; cook 5 minutes on each side or until desired degree of doneness. Cut duck diagonally across the grain into thin slices; serve with sauce. Yield: 4 servings (serving size: 1 duck breast half and about 2 tablespoons sauce).

CALORIES 380 (23% from fat); FAT 9.5g (sat 2.6g, mono 3.7g, poly 1.2g); PROTEIN 34.2g; CARB 23.1g; FIBER 0.6g; CHOL 131mg; IRON 8.3mg; SODIUM 347mg; CALC 29mg

Quick Tip: Frozen rhubarb can be substituted if fresh is unavailable.

Menu   SERVES 4

Seared Duck Breast with Ginger-Rhubarb Sauce

....

Garlic-fontina polenta

Combine 2 cups 2% reduced-fat milk, ½ cup water, ½ teaspoon salt, ¼ teaspoon freshly ground black pepper, and 1 minced garlic clove in a medium saucepan; bring to a boil. Gradually add ⅔ cup instant polenta, stirring constantly with a whisk. Cook 2 minutes or until thick, stirring constantly. Remove from heat; stir in ½ cup shredded fontina cheese.

....

Steamed baby bok choy

....

Game Plan

1 While sauce simmers:
  • Prepare duck

2 While milk comes to a boil for polenta:
  • Steam bok choy

3 Finish polenta.

4 Slice duck.

Fish and Shellfish

Versatile, quick-cooking fish offers a light,
healthy option for weeknight fare.

Menu

Sweet-Spicy Glazed Salmon

Baked sweet potatoes with brown sugar–pecan butter
Pierce 4 (8-ounce) sweet potatoes with a fork. Microwave at HIGH 12 minutes or until done. Combine 2 tablespoons softened butter, 2 tablespoons brown sugar, and 1½ tablespoons finely chopped toasted pecans. Top each potato with about 1 tablespoon butter mixture.

Broccoli spears

Game Plan

1 While oven heats for salmon:
- Prepare glaze for salmon
- Scrub sweet potatoes
- Prepare butter mixture for sweet potatoes

2 While salmon cooks:
- Cook sweet potatoes
- Prepare broccoli

Quick Tip:

To toast nuts quickly, place them on a paper plate, and microwave at HIGH one to two minutes or until nuts smell toasted.

Sweet-Spicy Glazed Salmon

Chinese-style hot mustard has a sharp bite similar to that of wasabi. If you can't find it, use Dijon mustard or one teaspoon of a dry mustard such as Coleman's.

Total time: 22 minutes

- 3 tablespoons dark brown sugar
- 1 tablespoon low-sodium soy sauce
- 4 teaspoons Chinese-style hot mustard
- 1 teaspoon rice vinegar
- 4 (6-ounce) salmon fillets (about 1 inch thick)
- Cooking spray
- ¼ teaspoon salt
- ¼ teaspoon freshly ground black pepper

1. Preheat oven to 425°.

2. Combine first 4 ingredients in a saucepan; bring to a boil. Remove from heat.

3. Place fish on a foil-lined jelly-roll pan coated with cooking spray; sprinkle with salt and pepper. Bake at 425° for 10 minutes. Remove from oven.

4. Preheat broiler.

5. Brush sugar mixture over fish; broil 3 inches from heat 3 minutes or until fish flakes easily when tested with a fork or until desired degree of doneness. Yield: 4 servings (serving size: 1 fillet).

CALORIES 252 (37% from fat); FAT 10.3g (sat 2.3g, mono 4.4g, poly 2.5g); PROTEIN 27.7g; CARB 11g; FIBER 0.1g; CHOL 65mg; IRON 0.9mg; SODIUM 470mg; CALC 33mg

Menu

Shrimp Tacos

Corn and avocado salsa

Combine 2 cups fresh corn kernels (about 4 ears), ⅓ cup chopped peeled avocado, ¼ cup finely chopped red onion, 2 tablespoons chopped fresh cilantro, 1 tablespoon fresh lime juice, and ½ teaspoon salt in a medium bowl; toss gently.

Lemon sorbet

Game Plan

1 Peel and devein shrimp.

2 While cooking water for shrimp comes to a boil:
- Chop cilantro, avocado, jalapeño, and red onion
- Cut kernels off corn cobs
- Juice lime

3 While shrimp cooks:
- Chop tomato
- Chop green onions

Shrimp Tacos

Shredded rotisserie chicken or flaked, cooked fish also works well in these tacos.

Total time: 30 minutes

- 3 tablespoons black peppercorns
- 3 quarts water
- 1 tablespoon salt
- 1 teaspoon ground red pepper
- 2 limes, quartered
- 1 pound medium shrimp, peeled and deveined
- ½ cup coarsely chopped fresh cilantro
- ¼ cup fresh lime juice
- 1 tablespoon minced seeded jalapeño pepper
- 12 (6-inch) corn tortillas
- ¾ cup chopped peeled tomato
- ½ cup reduced-fat sour cream
- ½ cup chopped green onions

1. Place the peppercorns on a double layer of cheesecloth. Gather edges of cheesecloth together, and tie securely. Combine cheesecloth bag, water, salt, red pepper, and lime quarters in a Dutch oven. Bring to a boil; cook 2 minutes. Add shrimp; cook 2 minutes or until done. Drain. Discard cheesecloth bag and lime quarters.

2. Combine shrimp, fresh cilantro, lime juice, and jalapeño pepper, tossing well to coat. Heat tortillas according to package directions. Spoon ⅓ cup shrimp mixture into each tortilla; top each taco with 1 tablespoon of tomato, 2 teaspoons sour cream, and 2 teaspoons onions. Yield: 4 servings (serving size: 3 tacos).

CALORIES 358 (20% from fat); FAT 7.8g (sat 3g, mono 0.8g, poly 1.7g); PROTEIN 29.3g; CARB 43.6g; FIBER 5.1g; CHOL 188mg; IRON 4.1mg; SODIUM 612mg; CALC 250mg

Quick Tip: The salsa and tacos both call for chopped cilantro and fresh lime juice, so measure for both recipes at the same time.

Pan-Roasted Grouper with Provençal Vegetables

Use a broiler pan for both components of this recipe. The fennel-tomato mixture cooks in the bottom of the pan, helping to steam the fish on the rack above.

Total time: 32 minutes

 2 cups thinly sliced fennel bulb (about 1 medium bulb)
 2 tablespoons fresh orange juice
 1 (28-ounce) can whole tomatoes, drained and coarsely chopped
 16 picholine olives, pitted and chopped
 ½ teaspoon salt, divided
 ½ teaspoon black pepper, divided
 Cooking spray
 2 teaspoons olive oil
 1 garlic clove, minced
 4 (6-ounce) grouper fillets

1. Preheat oven to 450°.

2. Combine first 4 ingredients. Add ¼ teaspoon salt and ¼ teaspoon pepper; toss well. Spoon mixture into a broiler pan coated with cooking spray. Bake at 450° for 10 minutes; stir once.

3. Combine ¼ teaspoon salt, ¼ teaspoon pepper, oil, and garlic; brush evenly over fish. Remove pan from oven. Place fish on rack of pan coated with cooking spray; place rack over fennel mixture.

4. Bake at 450° for 10 minutes or until fish flakes easily when tested with a fork or until desired degree of doneness. Yield: 4 servings (serving size: 1 fillet and ¾ cup fennel mixture).

CALORIES 247 (25% from fat); FAT 6.9g (sat 0.7g, mono 3.4g, poly 2.1g); PROTEIN 33.6g; CARB 11.5g; FIBER 2.8g; CHOL 60mg; IRON 2.6mg; SODIUM 898mg; CALC 91mg

Quick Tip: To make pitting olives easier, mash each olive with the flat side of a knife—the pit will easily dislodge.

Menu SERVES 4

Pan-Roasted Grouper with Provençal Vegetables

Spinach-mushroom salad
Combine 6 cups torn spinach, 1 cup sliced mushrooms, and ½ cup thinly sliced red onion. Combine ⅓ cup fat-free ranch dressing, ¼ cup (1 ounce) grated fresh Parmesan cheese, and ½ teaspoon freshly ground black pepper; spoon over salad. Toss gently to combine.

French bread

Game Plan

1 While oven heats:
 • Prepare vegetable mixture for fish
 • Wash spinach for salad

2 While vegetable mixture bakes:
 • Prepare fish

3 While fish and vegetables bake:
 • Prepare salad

Menu   SERVES 4

**Salmon with
Orange-Fennel Sauce**

Rice pilaf

*Heat 2 teaspoons olive oil in a large nonstick
skillet over medium-high heat. Add 1 cup
chopped onion; sauté 5 minutes or until
tender. Stir in 1 cup uncooked long-grain
rice; sauté 1 minute. Add 2 cups water, ¹/₂
teaspoon salt, ¹/₄ teaspoon dried thyme, and
¹/₈ teaspoon black pepper; bring to a boil.
Cover, reduce heat, and simmer 20 minutes
or until water is absorbed. Remove from
heat; let stand 5 minutes. Fluff with a fork.
Stir in 1 tablespoon chopped fresh parsley.*

Sautéed snow peas

Game Plan

1 Prepare marinade.

2 While fish marinates:
  • Preheat broiler for fish
  • Cook rice pilaf

3 While fish cooks:
  • Cook reserved marinade
  • Sauté snow peas
  • Chop parsley for rice pilaf

Salmon with Orange-Fennel Sauce

The mild acidity of fresh orange juice tempers the richness of salmon. Be careful not
to marinate longer than 20 minutes; the citrus marinade can "cook" the fish. Crush
the fennel seeds with a mortar and pestle, or place them in a zip-top plastic bag on a
cutting board, and crush them with a heavy pan.

Total time: 40 minutes
(includes marinating)

  2   teaspoons grated orange rind
¹/₂ cup fresh orange juice
  1   teaspoon chopped fresh
      rosemary
  1   teaspoon fennel seeds, crushed
  4   (6-ounce) salmon fillets
Cooking spray
¹/₄ teaspoon salt
¹/₈ teaspoon black pepper

1. Place first 4 ingredients in a large
zip-top plastic bag; add fish. Seal and
marinate in refrigerator 20 minutes.

2. Prepare broiler.

3. Remove fish from bag; reserve marinade. Place fish, skin sides down, on a
broiler pan coated with cooking spray;
sprinkle with salt and pepper. Broil 10
minutes or until fish flakes easily when
tested with a fork or until desired degree of doneness.

4. Bring reserved marinade to a boil in
a small saucepan. Reduce heat, and
simmer 3 minutes. Serve sauce with
fish. Yield: 4 servings (serving size: 1
fillet and about 1 tablespoon sauce).

CALORIES 244 (39% from fat); FAT 10.7g (sat 2.5g, mono 4.7g, poly
2.5g); PROTEIN 31.3g; CARB 3.8g; FIBER 0.4g; CHOL 80mg; IRON
0.7mg; SODIUM 214mg; CALC 28mg

Quick Tip: You can prepare the marinade up to one day in advance;
refrigerate in an airtight container.

Halibut with Charmoula

Charmoula is a traditional Moroccan herb sauce used to season or marinate fish.

Total time: 23 minutes

SAUCE:

- 1 tablespoon olive oil
- 1 teaspoon paprika
- ½ teaspoon salt
- ½ teaspoon ground cumin
- ½ teaspoon black pepper
- 2 garlic cloves or 4 teaspoons bottled chopped garlic
- 1 cup loosely packed fresh flat-leaf parsley leaves
- 1 cup loosely packed fresh cilantro leaves
- 2 tablespoons capers
- 2 teaspoons grated lemon rind
- ¼ cup fresh lemon juice

FISH:

- 4 (6-ounce) halibut fillets (about 1 inch thick)
- ¼ teaspoon salt
- ¼ teaspoon black pepper
- Cooking spray

1. Preheat oven to 350°.

2. To prepare sauce, combine first 6 ingredients in a food processor, and process until garlic is finely chopped. Add parsley leaves, cilantro, capers, rind, and juice; pulse until herbs are coarsely chopped.

3. To prepare fish, sprinkle fish with ¼ teaspoon salt and ¼ teaspoon pepper. Place fish on a foil-lined baking sheet coated with cooking spray.

4. Bake at 350° for 15 minutes or until fish flakes easily when tested with a fork or until desired degree of doneness. Yield: 4 servings (serving size: 1 halibut fillet and 1 tablespoon sauce).

CALORIES 234 (29% from fat); FAT 7.6g (sat 1.1g, mono 3.8g, poly 1.6g); PROTEIN 36.6g; CARB 3.8g; FIBER 1.3g; CHOL 54mg; IRON 2.9mg; SODIUM 701mg; CALC 118mg

Quick Tip: Add ½ cup golden raisins to the couscous when you add the boiling water. The raisins will plump as the couscous cooks.

Menu

SERVES 4

Halibut with Charmoula

Couscous tossed with golden raisins

Frozen yogurt with spiced honey and walnuts

Place ½ cup honey and ¼ teaspoon pumpkin-pie spice in a microwave-safe bowl. Microwave at HIGH 30 seconds or until warm. Spoon ½ cup vanilla fat-free frozen yogurt into each of 4 bowls, and top each serving with 2 tablespoons spiced honey and 1½ teaspoons of chopped toasted walnuts.

Game Plan

1 While oven heats:
- Prepare sauce

2 While fish bakes:
- Prepare couscous
- Scoop frozen yogurt into bowls, and place in freezer
- Toast walnuts for dessert
- Combine honey and spice (microwave after dinner)

Menu **SERVES 4**

Asian Flounder

Spinach and mandarin orange salad

Place 2 cups fresh torn spinach on each of 4 plates. Arrange ½ cup sliced mushrooms and ⅓ cup drained canned mandarin oranges over spinach. Sprinkle each serving with 1 tablespoon crumbled blue cheese and 1½ teaspoons chopped pecans; drizzle each with 2 tablespoons fat-free raspberry vinaigrette.

Quick-cooking brown rice

Game Plan

1 While water comes to a boil for the rice:
- Prepare ingredients for flounder and salad
- Measure ingredients for salad

2 While rice steams:
- Cook fish

3 Assemble salads.

Asian Flounder

Since fillets of flounder are usually quite thin, they often end up overcooked and dry when baked or sautéed. Steaming the fish in the microwave cooks it quickly so that it stays moist. The unusual method of folding and arranging the fish is necessary because the food toward the edge of the dish will cook more rapidly than that in the center.

Total time: 25 minutes

8 green onions
¼ cup minced fresh cilantro
1½ tablespoons minced peeled fresh ginger
2 teaspoons dark sesame oil, divided
4 (6-ounce) flounder or sole fillets
2 teaspoons rice vinegar
2 teaspoons low-sodium soy sauce
⅛ teaspoon salt
4 lemon slices

1. Remove green tops from onions; slice onion tops into 1-inch pieces to measure ¼ cup, and set aside. Reserve the remaining onion tops for another use. Cut white portions of onions into 2-inch pieces.

2. Combine cilantro, ginger, and 1 teaspoon oil in a 9-inch pie plate. Fold each fillet in half crosswise. Arrange fish spokelike, with thin portions pointing to center of dish. Arrange white onion portions between fillets. Combine ¼ cup green onion tops, 1 teaspoon oil, vinegar, soy sauce, and salt; pour over fish. Cover with plastic wrap. Microwave at HIGH 4 minutes or until the fish flakes easily when tested with a fork or until desired degree of doneness. Serve with lemon. Yield: 4 servings (serving size: 1 fillet).

CALORIES 188 (21% from fat); FAT 4.4g (sat 0.8g, mono 1.3g, poly 1.5g); PROTEIN 32.8g; CARB 2.7g; FIBER 0.9g; CHOL 82mg; IRON 1.3mg; SODIUM 299mg; CALC 57mg

Quick Tip: Quick-cooking brown rice complements the nutty flavor of the pecans in the salad and adds a pleasing color to the plate.

Sweet Black Pepper Fish

For most of its flavor, this Vietnamese classic relies on sugar and pepper, which most have on hand. The sugar makes a slightly bitter caramel sauce with fabulous results.

Total time: 23 minutes

½   cup water, divided
3   tablespoons sugar
2½ tablespoons Thai fish sauce
3   tablespoons minced peeled fresh
    lemongrass
1   tablespoon minced garlic
1   teaspoon freshly ground black
    pepper
1   cup chopped green onions
4   (6-ounce) halibut fillets
1   tablespoon chopped fresh
    cilantro

1. Combine ¼ cup water, sugar, and fish sauce in a large nonstick skillet; bring to a boil, stirring to dissolve the sugar. Add lemongrass, garlic, and pepper. Cook 1½ minutes or until slightly reduced.

2. Add ¼ cup water, green onions, and fish; cook over medium-high heat 7 minutes or until fish flakes easily when tested with a fork or until desired degree of doneness, turning once. Sprinkle with cilantro. Yield: 4 servings (serving size: 1 fillet and 2 tablespoons sauce).

CALORIES 247 (14% from fat); FAT 3.9g (sat 0.6g, mono 1.3g, poly 1.3g); PROTEIN 36.3g; CARB 13.9g; FIBER 1.2g; CHOL 54mg; IRON 1.9mg; SODIUM 911mg; CALC 89mg

Quick Tip: Lemongrass is a popular herb used in Thai cooking. It is shaped like green onions, but only the pale bottom part should be used.

Menu   SERVES 4

Sweet Black Pepper Fish
. . . .
Snow pea and red pepper stir-fry
Heat 1 teaspoon canola oil and ½ teaspoon dark sesame oil in a large nonstick skillet over medium-high heat. Add 1 teaspoon minced peeled fresh ginger and 2 minced garlic cloves; stir-fry 30 seconds. Add 2 cups trimmed snow peas, 1 cup red bell pepper strips, and ¼ teaspoon salt; stir-fry 3 minutes or until crisp-tender. Drizzle with 2 teaspoons low-sodium soy sauce; stir to coat.
. . . .
Steamed basmati rice
. . . .

Game Plan

1 While water boils for rice:
 • Prepare ingredients for fish and stir-fry

2 While rice cooks:
 • Prepare sauce for fish

3 While fish cooks:
 • Prepare stir-fry

Menu

SERVES 4

**Cornflake-Crusted Halibut with
Chile-Cilantro Aioli**

Oven fries

*Cut 2 large Yukon gold potatoes into ½ x
1-inch sticks; toss with 2 teaspoons olive
oil, and spread in a single layer on a baking
sheet lightly coated with cooking spray.
Bake at 450° for 30 minutes or until
golden, turning after 15 minutes. Toss with
½ teaspoon salt; serve immediately.*

Cabbage salad

Game Plan

1 While oven heats:
- Prepare aioli
- Cut potatoes
- Combine milk and egg white
- Prepare cornflake mixture

2 While potatoes cook:
- Prepare fish
- Toss salad

Cornflake-Crusted Halibut with Chile-Cilantro Aioli

Serve with the mayonnaise-based aioli and lemon wedges. To crush the cornflakes,
place them in a zip-top plastic bag, seal, and press with a rolling pin.

Total time: 25 minutes

AIOLI:

2 tablespoons minced fresh
   cilantro
3 tablespoons fat-free mayonnaise
1 serrano chile, seeded and
   minced
1 garlic clove, minced

FISH:

1 cup fat-free milk
1 large egg white, lightly
   beaten
2 cups cornflakes, finely crushed
¼ cup all-purpose flour
½ teaspoon salt
¼ teaspoon black pepper
2 tablespoons olive oil
4 (6-ounce) halibut fillets

1. To prepare aioli, combine first 4 ingredients, stirring well.

2. To prepare fish, combine milk and egg white in a shallow dish; stir well with a whisk. Combine cornflakes, flour, salt, and pepper in a shallow dish.

3. Heat oil in a large nonstick skillet over medium-high heat. Dip fish in milk mixture; dredge in cornflake mixture. Add fish to pan; cook 4 minutes on each side or until fish flakes easily when tested with a fork or until desired degree of doneness. Yield: 4 servings (serving size: 1 fish fillet and about 1 tablespoon aioli).

CALORIES 367 (27% from fat); FAT 11.2g (sat 1.6g, mono 6.3g, poly 1.9g); PROTEIN 40.8g; CARB 25.1g; FIBER 2.2g; CHOL 56mg; IRON 2.4mg; SODIUM 645mg; CALC 166mg

Quick Tip: As an alternative, use packaged potato wedges from the refrigerated section of the grocery store to make the oven fries.

Southern Shrimp and Grits

This Carolina Lowcountry specialty, or "breakfast shrimp," is great anytime. Use frozen bell pepper and onion, and prepeeled, deveined shrimp to minimize prep time.

Total time: 33 minutes

- 3 tablespoons fresh lemon juice
- ½ teaspoon hot pepper sauce
- 1½ pounds peeled and deveined large shrimp
- 2 bacon slices, chopped
- 1 cup chopped onion
- ¼ cup chopped green bell pepper
- 1½ teaspoons bottled minced garlic
- 1 cup fat-free, less-sodium chicken broth
- ½ cup chopped green onions, divided
- 5 cups water
- 1½ cups quick-cooking grits
- 1 tablespoon butter
- 1 teaspoon salt
- ¾ cup (3 ounces) shredded sharp cheddar cheese

1. Combine the first 3 ingredients, and set aside.

2. Cook bacon in a large nonstick skillet over medium heat until crisp. Add onion, bell pepper, and garlic to drippings in pan; cook 5 minutes or until tender, stirring occasionally. Stir in shrimp mixture, broth, and ¼ cup green onions; cook 5 minutes or until shrimp are done, stirring frequently.

3. Bring water to a boil in a medium saucepan; gradually add grits, stirring constantly. Reduce heat to low; simmer, covered, 5 minutes or until thick, stirring occasionally. Stir in butter and salt. Serve shrimp mixture over grits; sprinkle with cheese and onions. Yield: 6 servings (serving size: ⅔ cup shrimp mixture, ⅔ cup grits, 2 tablespoons cheese, and 2 teaspoons onions).

CALORIES 408 (28% from fat); FAT 12.5g (sat 5.6g, mono 4.1g, poly 1.3g); PROTEIN 32.8g; CARB 39.9g; FIBER 2g; CHOL 246mg; IRON 5.1mg; SODIUM 890mg; CALC 154mg

Quick Tip: Quick-cooking grits are a welcome weeknight alternative to stone-ground versions, which can take 45 minutes to cook.

Menu

SERVES 6

Southern Shrimp and Grits

Green salad with avocado and tomatoes

Combine 4 cups chopped romaine lettuce, 1 cup halved cherry tomatoes, ½ cup thinly vertically sliced red onion, and 1 sliced ripe avocado. Combine 2 tablespoons fresh lime juice, 2 teaspoons extravirgin olive oil, 1 teaspoon bottled minced garlic, ¼ teaspoon salt, and ¼ teaspoon black pepper, stirring with a whisk. Drizzle dressing over salad; toss gently to coat.

Orange sorbet

Game Plan

1 Prepare salad; cover and chill until serving time.

2 While water for grits comes to a boil:
- Combine shrimp, lemon juice, and hot sauce
- Chop bacon and green onions
- Shred cheese

3 While shrimp mixture cooks:
- Cook grits

Menu

SERVES 4

Trout with Lentils

Mixed greens salad with goat cheese croutons

Spread 2 teaspoons goat cheese onto each of 8 (1-ounce) French bread baguette slices; broil 1 minute. Combine 2 teaspoons extravirgin olive oil, 2 teaspoons sherry vinegar, 1 teaspoon honey, ¼ teaspoon salt, and ⅛ teaspoon freshly ground black pepper, stirring with a whisk. Toss 4 cups mixed salad greens with vinegar mixture; serve with cheese croutons.

Angel food cake with lemon curd

Game Plan

1 While lentils cook:
- Chop celery and parsley
- Preheat broiler

2 Broil trout.

3 While cheese croutons broil:
- Stir trout into lentil mixture
- Toss salad

Trout with Lentils

Serve this dish warm or as a chilled salad over a bed of greens. If you purchase smoked trout, the recipe will come together even faster.

Total time: 42 minutes

- 1 teaspoon olive oil
- ¼ cup chopped leek
- ¼ cup finely chopped carrot
- 2 garlic cloves, minced
- 1 cup dried lentils
- ½ cup water
- 1 (14-ounce) can fat-free, less-sodium chicken broth
- ¼ cup chopped celery
- 1 tablespoon chopped fresh parsley
- 1 tablespoon sherry vinegar
- ¾ teaspoon salt, divided
- ¼ teaspoon black pepper, divided
- 2 (6-ounce) trout fillets
- Cooking spray

1. Heat oil in a medium saucepan over medium-high heat. Add chopped leek, carrot, and garlic; sauté 2 minutes. Stir in lentils, water, and broth; bring to a boil. Cover, reduce heat, and simmer 25 minutes or until lentils are tender. Remove from heat. Add celery, parsley, vinegar, ½ teaspoon salt, and ⅛ teaspoon pepper, stirring to combine.

2. Preheat broiler.

3. Sprinkle trout with remaining ¼ teaspoon salt and ⅛ teaspoon pepper. Place fish on a baking sheet coated with cooking spray; broil 5 minutes or until fish flakes easily when tested with a fork or until desired degree of doneness. Break fish into chunks; add to lentil mixture, tossing gently. Yield: 4 servings (serving size: 1 cup).

CALORIES 311 (18% from fat); FAT 6.2g (sat 1.6g, mono 2.2g, poly 1.9g); PROTEIN 32.8g; CARB 31.3g; FIBER 15.2g; CHOL 50mg; IRON 5mg; SODIUM 668mg; CALC 96mg

Quick Tip: Pick up an angel food cake from the bakery, and pair it with prepared lemon curd, found with jams and jellies in the supermarket.

Pan-Seared Cod with Basil Sauce

If you have a minichopper, use it to make the basil sauce. Otherwise, take the time to chop the herb finely before stirring in the remaining ingredients.

Total time: 22 minutes

- ¼ cup fresh basil, minced
- ¼ cup fat-free, less-sodium chicken broth
- 2 tablespoons grated fresh Parmesan cheese
- 4 teaspoons extravirgin olive oil
- 1 teaspoon salt, divided
- 2 garlic cloves, minced
- 4 (6-ounce) cod fillets
- ¼ teaspoon freshly ground black pepper

Cooking spray

1. Combine minced basil, chicken broth, cheese, olive oil, ½ teaspoon of salt, and minced garlic in a small bowl.

2. Sprinkle fish with remaining ½ teaspoon salt and black pepper. Heat a large nonstick skillet over medium-high heat. Coat pan with cooking spray. Add fish; cook 5 minutes on each side or until fish flakes easily when tested with a fork or until desired degree of doneness. Serve fish with basil sauce. Yield: 4 servings (serving size: 1 fillet and about 1½ tablespoons sauce).

CALORIES 199 (30% from fat); FAT 6.6g (sat 1.3g, mono 3.5g, poly 0.8g); PROTEIN 32g; CARB 1.3g; FIBER 0.6g; CHOL 76mg; IRON 0.7mg; SODIUM 765mg; CALC 85mg

Quick Tip: To save time, use baby spinach, which won't require trimming the stems before cooking.

Menu   SERVES 4

Pan-Seared Cod with Basil Sauce

Garlic smashed potatoes
Place 4 cups cubed peeled Yukon gold potatoes in a saucepan; cover with water. Bring to a boil; cook 6 minutes or until tender. Drain. Return potatoes to pan. Add ¼ cup fat-free, less-sodium chicken broth, ¼ cup reduced-fat sour cream, 2 tablespoons butter, ½ teaspoon salt, and 3 minced garlic cloves; mash with a potato masher to desired consistency.

Sautéed spinach

Game Plan

1 While potatoes cook:
- Prepare basil sauce

2 While fish cooks:
- Finish potatoes
- Prepare spinach

Menu

SERVES 6

**Broiled Red Snapper with
Sicilian Tomato Pesto**

Asiago toast

*Place 6 (1½-ounce) slices Italian bread on
a baking sheet. Broil 1 minute on each side
or until toasted. Rub top of each bread slice
with cut side of a halved garlic clove. Drizzle
each slice with 1 teaspoon extravirgin olive
oil; sprinkle each slice with a dash of salt
and black pepper. Top each slice with 2
tablespoons grated Asiago cheese. Broil 1
minute or until cheese melts.*

Steamed green beans

Game Plan

1 Prepare pesto.

2 While water boils for orzo:
  • Preheat broiler

3 While orzo cooks:
  • Prepare fish
  • Steam green beans

4 Prepare toast.

Broiled Red Snapper with Sicilian Tomato Pesto

Plum tomatoes work best in this recipe; juicier tomatoes would thin the pesto.

Total time: 30 minutes

PESTO:

  2   cups basil leaves
  2   tablespoons pine nuts, toasted
  2   tablespoons extravirgin olive oil
  2   garlic cloves, minced
  ¼   cup (1 ounce) grated
      Parmigiano-Reggiano cheese
  ⅛   teaspoon crushed red pepper
1 ½   cups chopped plum tomato
  ½   teaspoon salt
  ½   teaspoon black pepper

FISH:

  6   (6-ounce) red snapper fillets
  ¼   teaspoon salt
Cooking spray

REMAINING INGREDIENT:

  3   cups hot cooked orzo
      (rice-shaped pasta)

1. To prepare pesto, combine first 4 ingredients in a food processor, and process until smooth. Add cheese and red pepper; process until blended. Combine basil puree, tomato, ½ teaspoon salt, and black pepper.

2. Preheat broiler.

3. To prepare fish, sprinkle with ¼ teaspoon salt. Arrange on a broiler pan coated with cooking spray, and broil 8 minutes or until fish flakes easily when tested with a fork or until desired degree of doneness. Serve with hot cooked orzo and pesto. Yield: 6 servings (serving size: 1 fillet, ½ cup orzo, and ¼ cup pesto).

CALORIES 437 (22% from fat); FAT 10.8g (sat 2.4g, mono 4.8g, poly 2g); PROTEIN 44.9g; CARB 38.9g; FIBER 3.1g; CHOL 67mg; IRON 2.9mg; SODIUM 497mg; CALC 156mg

Quick Tip: You can make the pesto ahead and keep it chilled.
Stir in the tomatoes just before serving.

Pecan-Crusted Tilapia

Total time: 25 minutes

- ½ cup dry breadcrumbs
- 2 tablespoons finely chopped pecans
- ½ teaspoon salt
- ¼ teaspoon garlic powder
- ¼ teaspoon black pepper
- ½ cup low-fat buttermilk
- ½ teaspoon hot sauce
- 3 tablespoons all-purpose flour
- 4 (6-ounce) tilapia or red snapper fillets
- 1 tablespoon vegetable oil, divided
- 4 lemon wedges

1. Combine first 5 ingredients in a shallow dish. Combine buttermilk and hot sauce in a medium bowl; place flour in a shallow dish. Dredge 1 fillet in flour. Dip in the buttermilk mixture; dredge in breadcrumb mixture. Repeat procedure with remaining fillets, flour, buttermilk, and breadcrumb mixtures.

2. Heat 1½ teaspoons oil in a large nonstick skillet over medium-high heat. Add 2 fillets; cook 3 minutes on each side or until fish flakes easily when tested with a fork or until desired degree of doneness. Repeat procedure with remaining oil and fillets. Serve with lemon wedges. Yield: 4 servings (serving size: 1 tilapia fillet).

CALORIES 302 (27% from fat); FAT 9.1g (sat 1.1g, mono 3.9g, poly 2.6g); PROTEIN 38.4g; CARB 14.2g; FIBER 0.9g; CHOL 64mg; IRON 1.3mg; SODIUM 530mg; CALC 98mg

Quick Tip: If you don't have buttermilk on hand, combine two teaspoons lemon juice and ½ cup low-fat milk; stir well.

Menu   SERVES 4

Pecan-Crusted Tilapia

Quick coleslaw
Combine 2 tablespoons white vinegar, 3 tablespoons low-fat mayonnaise, ½ teaspoon black pepper, and ⅛ teaspoon ground red pepper in a large bowl, stirring with a whisk. Add 5 cups cabbage coleslaw mix; toss well to coat.

Rice

Game Plan

1 Prepare coleslaw.

2 While water for rice comes to a boil:
- Prepare ingredients for fish

3 Cook rice.

4 While rice stands:
- Cook fish

Menu

Asian Marinated Striped Bass

Rice noodles

Soak 4 ounces rice noodles in warm water for 20 minutes. Drain; toss with 2 teaspoons peanut oil. Heat 2 teaspoons peanut oil in a large nonstick skillet over medium-high heat; sauté ½ cup thinly sliced shallots 1 minute. Add noodles to pan; cook 3 minutes or until thoroughly heated, tossing well. Stir in ¼ cup chopped green onions, ¼ cup chopped fresh cilantro, 1 tablespoon Thai fish sauce, and 2 teaspoons sugar. Top each serving with 1 teaspoon chopped peanuts.

Steamed baby bok choy

Game Plan

1 While fish marinates:
- Soak noodles
- Slice shallots
- Chop green onions, cilantro, and peanuts for noodles
- Steam bok choy, and keep warm

2 While fish cooks:
- Prepare rice noodles

Asian Marinated Striped Bass

Only four ingredients give this quick marinade a lot of flavor.

Total time: 33 minutes

- 2 tablespoons minced fresh cilantro
- 1 tablespoon sugar
- 3 tablespoons fish sauce
- 2 garlic cloves, minced
- 4 (6-ounce) striped bass fillets
- Cooking spray

1. Combine first 4 ingredients in a large zip-top plastic bag; add fish to bag. Seal and marinate in refrigerator 20 minutes, turning once. Remove fish from bag, reserving marinade.

2. Heat a large nonstick skillet over medium-high heat. Coat pan with cooking spray. Add fish to pan; cook 4 minutes on each side or until fish flakes easily when tested with a fork or until desired degree of doneness. Remove from pan. Add marinade to pan; bring to a boil. Cook 30 seconds; serve with fish. Yield: 4 servings (serving size: 1 fillet and 2 teaspoons sauce).

CALORIES 185 (19% from fat); FAT 4g (sat 0.9g, mono 1.1g, poly 1.3g); PROTEIN 31g; CARB 4.2g; FIBER 0.1g; CHOL 136mg; IRON 1.6mg; SODIUM 1,146mg; CALC 10mg

Quick Tip: If you can't find baby bok choy, you can steam Napa or Chinese cabbage instead.

Miso-Glazed Salmon

This sweet-salty miso, brown sugar, and soy sauce glaze caramelizes in about 10 minutes as it cooks atop this rich, meaty salmon.

Total time: 17 minutes

¼ cup packed brown sugar
2 tablespoons low-sodium soy sauce
2 tablespoons hot water
2 tablespoons miso (soybean paste)
4 (6-ounce) salmon fillets (about 1 inch thick)
Cooking spray
1 tablespoon chopped fresh chives

1. Preheat broiler.

2. Combine the first 4 ingredients. Arrange fish in a baking dish coated with cooking spray. Spoon miso mixture evenly over fish. Broil 10 minutes or until fish flakes easily when tested with a fork or until desired degree of doneness, basting twice with miso mixture. Top with chives. Yield: 4 servings.

CALORIES 297 (33% from fat); FAT 10.9g (sat 2.5g, mono 4.7g, poly 2.8g); PROTEIN 32.4g; CARB 15.7g; FIBER 0.3g; CHOL 80mg; IRON 1mg; SODIUM 742mg; CALC 29mg

Quick Tip: Place a steamer basket over the boiling potatoes; steam the peas and carrots during the last few minutes of the potatoes' cooking time.

Menu   SERVES 4

Miso-Glazed Salmon

Wasabi mashed potatoes
Place 2 pounds cubed red potato in a large saucepan; cover with water. Bring to a boil; cook 15 minutes or until tender. Drain. Place potato; ¼ cup fat-free, less-sodium chicken broth; ¼ cup reduced-fat sour cream; 2 tablespoons butter; 1 teaspoon wasabi paste; ½ teaspoon salt; and ¼ teaspoon black pepper in a bowl. Mash to desired consistency.

Snow peas and sliced carrots

Game Plan

1 While water comes to a boil for potato and oven heats for fish:
 • Prepare miso mixture for fish
 • Combine flavorings for mashed potatoes in a large bowl

2 While potato and fish cook:
 • Steam snow peas and carrots
 • Chop chives

Pasta

With a quick cook and a speedy sauce, you can have these pasta dishes on the table in no time.

PHOTOGRAPHY: HOWARD L. PUCKETT/STYLING: MELANIE J. CLARKE

Menu

Pasta Jambalaya

....

Mixed greens with Dijon vinaigrette
Combine ½ cup fat-free, less-sodium chicken broth; ½ cup balsamic vinegar; 2 tablespoons olive oil; 2 teaspoons Dijon mustard; 1 teaspoon anchovy paste; 3 minced garlic cloves; and ¼ teaspoon black pepper in a jar. Cover and shake vigorously. Drizzle ½ cup vinaigrette over 8 cups mixed salad greens; toss gently.

....

French bread

....

Game Plan

1 Prepare vinaigrette; refrigerate.

2 While water comes to a boil:
• Prepare ingredients for jambalaya

3 While pasta cooks:
• Prepare jambalaya

4 Toss salad.

Quick Tip: You can substitute the same amount of gemelli, small seashell pasta, or mostaccioli for penne.

Pasta Jambalaya

Try Monterey Jack with jalapeño peppers, colby-Jack, or cheddar in place of Mexican blend cheese, if you have one of them on hand.

Total time: 35 minutes

3 cups uncooked penne (tube-shaped pasta)
Cooking spray
½ cup chopped onion
½ cup chopped red bell pepper
1 garlic clove, minced
1 teaspoon Cajun seasoning
1 (15-ounce) can black beans, rinsed and drained

1 (10-ounce) can diced tomatoes and green chiles, undrained
3 ounces turkey kielbasa, halved lengthwise and thinly sliced
½ cup (2 ounces) preshredded reduced-fat 4-cheese Mexican blend cheese (such as Sargento)

1. Cook pasta according to package directions, omitting salt and fat. Drain and set aside.
2. While the pasta cooks, heat a large nonstick skillet over medium-high heat. Coat pan with cooking spray. Add onion, bell pepper, and garlic; sauté 5 minutes. Add seasoning; sauté 1 minute. Add beans, tomatoes, and kielbasa; bring to a boil. Reduce heat, and simmer until thick (about 10 minutes). Combine bean mixture and pasta in a large bowl. Top with cheese. Yield: 6 servings (serving size: 1⅓ cups).

CALORIES 263 (15% from fat); FAT 4.3g (sat 2.1g, mono 0.9g, poly 0.6g); PROTEIN 11.7g; CARB 43.9g; FIBER 3.8g; CHOL 12mg; IRON 3.7mg; SODIUM 419mg; CALC 86mg

Menu

SERVES 4

**Fettuccine with Shrimp
and Portobellos**

....

Arugula salad

*Combine 1 tablespoon fresh lemon juice,
2 teaspoons extravirgin olive oil, ¼
teaspoon kosher salt, ⅛ teaspoon cracked
black pepper, and 1 minced garlic clove.
Place 1½ cups arugula on each of 4 salad
plates. Drizzle dressing evenly over
salads. Shave 1 ounce fresh Parmesan
cheese; divide evenly among salads.*

....

French baguette

....

Game Plan

1 While water comes to a boil:
  • Peel and devein shrimp
  • Clean and slice mushroom
  • Chop onion and garlic

2 While pasta cooks:
  • Cook mushroom mixture
  • Prepare salad
  • Shred cheese

Fettuccine with Shrimp and Portobellos

Serve this entrée in a bowl with toasted bread to soak up the flavorful broth.

Total time: 30 minutes

  8 ounces uncooked fettuccine
  1 (4-inch) portobello mushroom
     cap (about 5 ounces)
  1 tablespoon olive oil
  1 cup finely chopped onion
  ¼ cup chopped fresh flat-leaf
     parsley
  ¼ teaspoon salt
  1 garlic clove, minced
  1 cup fat-free, less-sodium chicken
     broth
  ¼ cup dry white wine
  ¾ pound large shrimp, peeled and
     deveined
  ½ cup (2 ounces) shredded Asiago
     cheese
  1 tablespoon chopped fresh chives

1. Cook pasta according to package
directions, omitting salt and fat. Drain
and rinse under cold water. Drain.

2. Remove brown gills from underside
of mushroom cap using a spoon; discard gills. Cut cap into thin slices. Cut
slices in half crosswise.

3. Heat olive oil in a large saucepan
over medium-high heat. Add mushroom, onion, parsley, salt, and garlic;
sauté 4 minutes or until mushroom re-
leases moisture, stirring frequently.
Stir in broth, wine, and shrimp; bring
to a boil. Add pasta; cook 3 minutes or
until shrimp are done, tossing to combine. Sprinkle with cheese and chives.
Yield: 4 servings (serving size: 1¾
cups shrimp mixture, 2 tablespoons
cheese, and about 1 teaspoon chives).

CALORIES 384 (21% from fat); FAT 9.1g (sat 3.3g, mono 2.7g, poly
0.9g); PROTEIN 23.8g; CARB 48.9g; FIBER 2.8g; CHOL 114mg;
IRON 4.5mg; SODIUM 540mg; CALC 156mg

Quick Tip: Mince the garlic for the pasta and salad at the same time.

Udon-Beef Noodle Bowl

This entrée falls somewhere between a soup and a noodle dish. You can eat it with chopsticks, but be sure to have a spoon to catch the broth.

Total time: 35 minutes

- 8 ounces uncooked udon noodles (thick, round fresh Japanese wheat noodles) or spaghetti
- 1½ teaspoons bottled minced garlic
- ½ teaspoon crushed red pepper
- 2 (14-ounce) cans less-sodium beef broth
- 3 tablespoons low-sodium soy sauce
- 3 tablespoons sake (rice wine) or dry sherry
- 1 tablespoon honey
- Cooking spray
- 2 cups sliced shiitake mushroom caps (about 4 ounces)
- ½ cup thinly sliced carrot
- 8 ounces top round, thinly sliced
- ¾ cup diagonally cut green onions
- 1 (6-ounce) package fresh baby spinach

1. Cook noodles according to package directions; drain.

2. Place garlic, pepper, and broth in a large saucepan. Bring to a boil; reduce heat, and simmer 10 minutes.

3. Combine soy sauce, sake, and honey in a small bowl; stir with a whisk.

4. Heat a large nonstick skillet over medium-high heat. Coat pan with cooking spray. Add mushrooms and carrot, and sauté 2 minutes. Stir in soy sauce mixture; cook 2 minutes, stirring constantly. Add vegetable mixture to broth mixture. Stir in beef; cook 2 minutes or until beef loses its pink color. Stir in noodles, green onions, and spinach. Serve immediately. Yield: 5 servings (serving size: about 1½ cups).

CALORIES 306 (16% from fat); FAT 5.6g (sat 1.8g, mono 2g, poly 0.4g); PROTEIN 22.4g; CARB 36.6g; FIBER 2.4g; CHOL 39mg; IRON 3.4mg; SODIUM 707mg; CALC 59mg

Quick Tip: To speed the slicing of the shiitakes, stack a few caps on top of one another, then slice the entire stack.

Menu   SERVES 5

Udon-Beef Noodle Bowl

Steamed edamame

Gingered wonton chips with ice cream

Cut 10 wonton wrappers into thin strips. Combine wonton strips and ½ teaspoon dark sesame oil in a small bowl, tossing to coat. Add 2 teaspoons sugar and ½ teaspoon ground ginger, tossing to coat. Arrange strips on a baking sheet. Bake at 400° for 8 minutes or until crisp, turning once. Serve wonton chips with vanilla low-fat ice cream.

Game Plan

1 Heat oven.

2 While water comes to a boil:
- Prepare wontons for baking
- Slice mushrooms, carrot, and beef

3 While noodles cook and broth mixture simmers:
- Bake wonton chips
- Steam edamame
- Sauté vegetables for noodle bowl

Menu
SERVES 6

Turkey Tetrazzini

Green beans with almonds
Trim 1 pound green beans; cook in boiling water 2 minutes or until crisp-tender. Drain. Toast 2 tablespoons sliced almonds in a nonstick skillet over medium-high heat 2 minutes, stirring frequently. Add 2 teaspoons butter to pan; cook 30 seconds or until lightly browned. Add green beans, ½ teaspoon salt, and ¼ teaspoon black pepper, tossing to coat.

Garlic bread

Game Plan

1 While water comes to a boil for pasta and green beans:
- Trim green beans
- Heat skillet for turkey
- Preheat oven

2 While pasta and beans cook:
- Cook turkey
- Cook mushroom mixture

3 While casserole bakes:
- Prepare garlic bread
- Toast almonds
- Finish green beans

Turkey Tetrazzini

This is a great recipe to make ahead and refrigerate; bake just before you're ready to serve it. Chicken breasts pounded to ¼-inch thickness are an option for the cutlets.

Total time: 43 minutes

- 10 ounces uncooked vermicelli
- 2 teaspoons vegetable oil
- 1 pound turkey breast cutlets
- ¾ teaspoon onion powder, divided
- ½ teaspoon salt, divided
- ¼ teaspoon black pepper, divided
- 2 tablespoons dry sherry
- 2 (8-ounce) packages presliced mushrooms
- ¾ cup frozen green peas, thawed
- ¾ cup fat-free milk
- ⅔ cup fat-free sour cream
- ⅓ cup (about 1½ ounces) grated fresh Parmesan cheese
- 1 (10¾-ounce) can reduced-fat cream of chicken soup
- Cooking spray
- ⅓ cup dry breadcrumbs
- 2 tablespoons butter, melted

1. Preheat oven to 450°.

2. Cook pasta according to package directions, omitting salt and fat. Drain and set aside.

3. Heat oil in a large nonstick skillet over medium-high heat. Sprinkle the turkey with ½ teaspoon onion powder, ¼ teaspoon salt, and ⅛ teaspoon pepper. Add turkey to pan, and cook 2 minutes on each side or until done. Remove turkey from pan.

4. Add ¼ teaspoon onion powder, sherry, and mushrooms to pan. Cover and cook for 4 minutes or until mushrooms are tender.

5. Combine peas, milk, sour cream, cheese, and soup in a large bowl. Chop turkey. Add the remaining ¼ teaspoon salt, ⅛ teaspoon pepper, pasta, turkey, and mushroom mixture to soup mixture, tossing gently to combine. Spoon mixture into a 13 x 9–inch baking dish coated with cooking spray.

6. Combine breadcrumbs and butter in a small dish, tossing to combine. Sprinkle breadcrumb mixture over pasta mixture. Bake at 450° for 12 minutes or until bubbly and thoroughly heated. Yield: 6 servings (serving size: about 1⅔ cups).

CALORIES 459 (29% from fat); FAT 14.8g (sat 5.9g, mono 4.4g, poly 2.8g); PROTEIN 30.5g; CARB 48.1g; FIBER 3.1g; CHOL 69mg; IRON 4mg; SODIUM 716mg; CALC 199mg

Quick Tip: Heat the garlic bread in the oven with the casserole so everything will be ready at the same time.

Shrimp Pad Thai

Pad thai is the most popular noodle dish in Thailand. Pungent fish sauce (also called *nam pla*) is an important flavoring for this dish; you can find it in the Asian foods section of most large supermarkets or in Asian markets. Substitute four cups hot cooked linguine for the rice stick noodles if you have trouble finding them.

Total time: 30 minutes

- 8 ounces wide rice stick noodles (*banh pho*)
- ¼ cup ketchup
- 2 tablespoons sugar
- 3 tablespoons fish sauce
- ½ teaspoon crushed red pepper
- 2 tablespoons canola oil, divided
- 1 pound medium shrimp, peeled and deveined
- 2 large eggs, lightly beaten
- 1 cup fresh bean sprouts
- ¾ cup (1-inch) slices green onions
- 1 garlic clove, minced
- 2 tablespoons chopped unsalted, dry-roasted peanuts

1. Place noodles in a large bowl. Add hot water to cover; let stand 12 minutes or until tender. Drain.

2. Combine ketchup, sugar, fish sauce, and pepper in a small bowl.

3. Heat 2 teaspoons oil in a large non-stick skillet over medium-high heat. Add shrimp; sauté 2 minutes or until shrimp are done. Remove shrimp from pan; keep warm.

4. Heat 4 teaspoons oil in pan over medium-high heat. Add eggs; cook 30 seconds or until soft-scrambled, stirring constantly. Add sprouts, green onions, and garlic; cook for 1 minute. Add noodles, ketchup mixture, and shrimp; cook for 3 minutes or until heated. Sprinkle with peanuts. Yield: 6 servings (serving size: 1½ cups).

CALORIES 346 (25% from fat); FAT 9.3g (sat 1.3g, mono 4.3g, poly 2.6g); PROTEIN 22.2g; CARB 41.9g; FIBER 2.3g; CHOL 185mg; IRON 4mg; SODIUM 945mg; CALC 78mg

Menu   SERVES 6

Shrimp Pad Thai

Spicy cucumber salad

Combine 2 cups thinly sliced seeded peeled cucumber, 1 cup julienne-cut red bell pepper, and ¼ cup thinly sliced red onion in a large bowl. Combine 1 tablespoon sugar, 2 tablespoons fresh lime juice, 1 tablespoon fish sauce, and ½ teaspoon crushed red pepper in a small bowl. Pour dressing over vegetables; toss to combine.

Lemon sorbet

Game Plan

1 While water for noodles heats:
- Prepare cucumber salad

2 While noodles soak:
- Peel and devein shrimp
- Combine sauce ingredients
- Slice green onions
- Beat eggs

3 Prepare pad thai.

Quick Tip: You'll save time in the kitchen if you buy peeled and deveined shrimp. It may cost a bit more, but it's worth it if you're in a hurry. Buy more than you need, and freeze for future use.

Soups and Stews

These fast, flavorful, casual meals are hardworking choices for easy suppers.

PHOTOGRAPHY: BECKY LUIGART-STAYNER/STYLING: CINDY BARR

Menu

New England Clam Chowder

Red cabbage and apple slaw

Combine ½ cup fresh orange juice, ¼ cup reduced-fat sour cream, 1 tablespoon malt vinegar, ½ teaspoon caraway seeds, ¼ teaspoon kosher salt, and ¼ teaspoon freshly ground black pepper, stirring well with a whisk. Combine 5 cups thinly sliced red cabbage, 2 shredded Granny Smith apples, and 2 tablespoons chopped, toasted walnuts. Drizzle with orange juice mixture, and toss well to combine.

Oyster crackers

Game Plan

1 Chop and measure ingredients for soup.

2 Sauté onion mixture.

3 While potato mixture simmers:
- Prepare slaw dressing
- Shred cabbage and apples
- Chop and toast walnuts

4 Toss slaw.

Quick Tip:

Use a food processor's slicing and shredding blades to quickly prepare the cabbage and apples for the slaw.

New England Clam Chowder

Potatoes and milk add body to this recipe, made convenient with canned clams and bottled clam juice.

Total time: 30 minutes

- 2 teaspoons olive oil
- 1 cup diced onion
- ½ cup diced celery
- 2 cups (½-inch) cubed peeled Yukon gold or baking potato (about ¾ pound)
- 1 cup water
- ½ teaspoon dried thyme
- ⅛ teaspoon black pepper
- 1 (8-ounce) bottle clam juice
- 1 bay leaf
- 1 cup 2% reduced-fat milk
- 1 tablespoon all-purpose flour
- 1 (6½-ounce) can minced clams, undrained

1. Heat oil in a large saucepan over medium heat. Add onion and celery; sauté 5 minutes or until onion is tender. Stir in potato and next 5 ingredients (through bay leaf); bring to a boil. Cover, reduce heat, and simmer 12 minutes or until potato is tender.

2. Combine milk and flour in a small bowl, stirring with a whisk until smooth. Add flour mixture and clams to pan, and bring to a simmer. Cook 2 minutes or until the mixture begins to thicken, stirring frequently. Discard bay leaf. Yield: 4 servings (serving size: 1¼ cups).

CALORIES 184 (19% from fat); FAT 3.9g (sat 1.2g, mono 2.1g, poly 0.4g); PROTEIN 8.4g; CARB 28.5g; FIBER 2.5g; CHOL 20mg; IRON 2.7mg; SODIUM 434mg; CALC 132mg

Menu SERVES 4

Twenty-Minute Chili

Mango-avocado salad

*Combine 2½ cups chopped peeled ripe
mango, 1½ cups cherry tomato halves, ½
cup chopped peeled avocado, ¼ cup sliced
green onions, 2 tablespoons chopped fresh
cilantro, 2 tablespoons fresh lime juice, and
½ teaspoon salt; toss and chill.*

Corn bread sticks

Game Plan

1 Prepare salad; cover and chill.

2 Chop and measure ingredients
for chili.

3 While water comes to a boil
for rice:
- Heat oven for corn bread sticks

4 While rice steams:
- Bake corn bread sticks
- Prepare chili

Twenty-Minute Chili

Serving chili over rice is popular in Texas. We also recommend corn bread sticks.

Total time: 35 minutes

- 1 (3½-ounce) bag boil-in-bag long-grain rice
- 1 tablespoon vegetable oil
- 1 cup chopped onion
- ¾ cup chopped green bell pepper
- ½ pound ground turkey breast
- 1 tablespoon chili powder
- 1 teaspoon Worcestershire sauce
- ½ teaspoon ground cumin
- ½ teaspoon dried oregano
- ¼ teaspoon salt
- ¼ teaspoon black pepper
- 1 (15-ounce) can kidney beans, rinsed and drained
- 1 (14.5-ounce) can Mexican-style stewed tomatoes with jalapeño peppers and spices, undrained
- 1 (5.5-ounce) can tomato juice
- ¼ cup (1 ounce) preshredded reduced-fat cheddar cheese

1. Cook rice according to package directions, omitting salt and fat.
2. While rice cooks, heat oil in a large nonstick skillet over medium-high heat. Add onion, green bell pepper, and turkey; cook 3 minutes or until done, stirring to crumble. Stir in chili powder and the next 8 ingredients (through tomato juice); bring to a boil. Cover, reduce heat, and simmer 10 minutes. Serve over rice; sprinkle with cheese. Yield: 4 servings (serving size: 1¼ cups chili, ½ cup rice, and 1 tablespoon cheese).

CALORIES 380 (26% from fat); FAT 10.5g (sat 2.8g, mono 2.6g, poly 3.3g); PROTEIN 21.4g; CARB 51g; FIBER 11.2g; CHOL 50mg; IRON 4mg; SODIUM 739mg; CALC 125mg

Quick Tip: If you can't find ripe mangoes, bottled sliced mango can be substituted. Look for it in the refrigerated aisle where jarred orange and grapefruit sections are displayed.

Chicken and Barley Stew

Frozen chopped onion makes this dish even quicker to prepare. If you use it, add with the frozen mixed vegetables.

Total time: 30 minutes

- 1 cup uncooked quick-cooking barley
- 3 (14-ounce) cans fat-free, less-sodium chicken broth
- 1 tablespoon olive oil
- 1¾ cups chopped onion
- 1 (10-ounce) package frozen mixed vegetables
- 1 cup chopped cooked chicken
- ¼ teaspoon salt
- ¼ teaspoon dried thyme
- ¼ teaspoon black pepper

1. Bring barley and broth to a boil in a large saucepan. Reduce heat, and simmer 5 minutes.

2. While barley cooks, heat oil in a large nonstick skillet over medium-high heat. Add onion; sauté 3 minutes. Add mixed vegetables; sauté 2 minutes. Add vegetable mixture, chicken, salt, thyme, and pepper to barley mixture; simmer 4 minutes. Yield: 4 servings (serving size: about 1¾ cups).

CALORIES 356 (19% from fat); FAT 7.5g (sat 1.5g, mono 1.9g, poly 3.3g); PROTEIN 22.7g; CARB 50.7g; FIBER 12.1g; CHOL 31mg; IRON 3.1mg; SODIUM 763mg; CALC 54mg

Quick Tip: Purchase packaged prewashed torn romaine to save time.

Menu   SERVES 4

Chicken and Barley Stew

Romaine salad

Combine 2 tablespoons light mayonnaise, 1 tablespoon Dijon mustard, 2 teaspoons fresh lemon juice, 1 teaspoon red wine vinegar, ½ teaspoon Worcestershire sauce, and 2 minced garlic cloves in a large bowl, stirring with a whisk. Add 8 cups torn romaine lettuce, tossing gently to coat.

Water crackers

Game Plan

1 Chop and measure ingredients for stew.

2 Prepare salad dressing; tear lettuce.

3 While barley simmers:
  • Cook vegetables for soup

4 While stew simmers:
  • Toss salad

Menu SERVES 4

Creamy Potato-Mushroom Soup

Romaine, strawberry, and lemon salad

Combine 5 cups torn romaine lettuce, 1 1/2 cups sliced strawberries, and 1/2 cup thinly vertically sliced red onion in a large bowl. Combine 2 tablespoons fresh lemon juice, 1 tablespoon honey, 2 teaspoons extravirgin olive oil, 1 teaspoon Dijon mustard, 1/4 teaspoon salt, and 1/4 teaspoon black pepper, stirring with a whisk. Drizzle dressing over salad, and toss gently to coat. Sprinkle with 1/4 cup shaved Parmesan cheese.

Breadsticks

Game Plan

1 Chop and measure ingredients for soup.

2 While soup simmers:
  • Prepare salad

Creamy Potato-Mushroom Soup

Total time: 40 minutes

  2 bacon slices
  4 cups chopped cremini mushrooms
 1/2 cup chopped shallots
3 1/2 cups cubed Yukon gold or baking potato
  1 (14-ounce) can fat-free, less-sodium chicken broth
  2 cups 1% low-fat milk
  2 tablespoons sherry
 1/2 teaspoon salt
 1/4 teaspoon black pepper

1. Cook bacon in a Dutch oven over medium heat until crisp. Remove bacon from pan; crumble and set aside. Add mushrooms and shallots to bacon drippings in pan; sauté 5 minutes or until the mushrooms are soft. Remove from pan; set aside.

2. Add potato and broth to pan; bring to a boil. Cover, reduce heat, and simmer 12 minutes or until potato is very tender. Place potato mixture in a food processor or blender, and process until smooth. Return the potato mixture to the pan.

3. Add low-fat milk, mushroom mixture, sherry, salt, and pepper; cook over low heat 10 minutes or until thoroughly heated. Ladle soup into bowls, and top with crumbled bacon. Yield: 4 servings (serving size: 1 1/2 cups).

CALORIES 236 (13% from fat); FAT 3.5g (sat 1.5g, mono 1.2g, poly 0.4g); PROTEIN 13.2g; CARB 39.4g; FIBER 3.3g; CHOL 9mg; IRON 2.4mg; SODIUM 521mg; CALC 172mg

Quick Tip: To make cheese shavings, run a sharp vegetable peeler over a piece of fresh Parmesan cheese.

Spicy Mulligatawny

The name of this highly seasoned Indian soup means "pepper water." It gets quite a kick from the combination of curry powder, ground ginger, and crushed red pepper, but you can halve those ingredients if you don't like spicy foods.

Total time: 35 minutes

- 1 tablespoon vegetable oil, divided
- ½ pound skinless, boneless chicken breast, cut into bite-sized pieces
- 1 cup chopped peeled Gala or Braeburn apple
- ¾ cup chopped onion
- ½ cup chopped carrot
- ½ cup chopped celery
- ½ cup chopped green bell pepper
- 2 tablespoons all-purpose flour
- 1 tablespoon curry powder
- 1 teaspoon ground ginger
- ½ teaspoon crushed red pepper
- ¼ teaspoon salt
- 2 (14-ounce) cans fat-free, less-sodium chicken broth
- ⅓ cup mango chutney
- ¼ cup tomato paste

Chopped fresh parsley (optional)

1. Heat 1 teaspoon of oil in a Dutch oven over medium-high heat. Add chicken, and sauté 3 minutes. Remove from pan; set aside.

2. Heat 2 teaspoons oil in pan. Add apple and next 4 ingredients (through bell pepper); sauté 5 minutes, stirring frequently. Stir in flour and the next 4 ingredients (through salt), and cook 1 minute. Stir in broth, chutney, and tomato paste; bring to a boil. Reduce heat; simmer 8 minutes.

3. Return chicken to pan, and cook 2 minutes or until mixture is thoroughly heated. Sprinkle with parsley, if desired. Yield: 4 servings (serving size: 1¼ cups).

CALORIES 236 (18% from fat); FAT 4.8g (sat 0.8g, mono 1.1g, poly 2.3g); PROTEIN 18g; CARB 31g; FIBER 4.9g; CHOL 33mg; IRON 1.9mg; SODIUM 599mg; CALC 42mg

Menu   SERVES 4

Spicy Mulligatawny

Pita wedges

Ice cream with sautéed pears
Toss 2 cups sliced peeled pear with 1 teaspoon lemon juice. Heat 1 tablespoon butter in a nonstick skillet over medium-high heat. Add pear; sauté 6 minutes or until tender. Stir in 2 tablespoons brown sugar. Serve pear over vanilla low-fat ice cream; top with crushed gingersnaps.

Game Plan

1 Chop and measure ingredients for soup.

2 While soup simmers:
- Sauté pear for dessert; keep warm
- Crush gingersnaps for dessert
- Cut pitas into wedges

Quick Tip: Slightly frozen chicken cuts quickly and easily. Place raw chicken in the freezer for 20 minutes before cutting into bite-sized pieces.

Menu

Quick Fall Minestrone

Monterey Jack and roasted red pepper quesadillas

Place 8 (6-inch) fat-free flour tortillas on a large baking sheet coated with cooking spray. Sprinkle each tortilla evenly with 2 tablespoons shredded Monterey Jack cheese and 2 tablespoons chopped bottled roasted red bell peppers. Top each tortilla with another (6-inch) fat-free flour tortilla; coat tops with cooking spray. Broil 3 minutes or until lightly browned. Carefully turn over; coat tops with cooking spray. Broil an additional 3 minutes or until lightly browned. Cut each quesadilla into 4 wedges; serve 4 wedges per person.

Cantaloupe, grape, and honeydew fruit salad

Game Plan

1 While broiler heats for quesadillas:
- Chop vegetables for soup
- Shred cheese for quesadillas
- Chop bell peppers for quesadillas

2 While soup cooks:
- Broil quesadillas
- Grate cheese for soup

Quick Fall Minestrone

This easy soup brims with fresh vegetables; canned beans and orzo make it hearty and filling. Use a vegetable peeler to quickly remove the skin from the squash.

Total time: 35 minutes

- 1 tablespoon vegetable oil
- 1 cup chopped onion
- 2 garlic cloves, minced
- 6 cups vegetable broth
- 2½ cups (¾-inch) cubed peeled butternut squash
- 2½ cups (¾-inch) cubed peeled baking potato
- 1 cup (1-inch) cut green beans (about ¼ pound)
- ½ cup diced carrot
- 1 teaspoon dried oregano
- ¼ teaspoon black pepper
- ¼ teaspoon salt
- 4 cups chopped kale
- ½ cup uncooked orzo (rice-shaped pasta)
- 1 (16-ounce) can cannellini beans or other white beans, rinsed and drained
- ½ cup (2 ounces) grated fresh Parmesan cheese

1. Heat oil in a large Dutch oven over medium-high heat. Add onion and garlic; sauté 2½ minutes. Add broth and next 7 ingredients (through salt); bring to a boil. Reduce heat; simmer 3 minutes. Add kale, orzo, and cannellini beans; cook 5 minutes or until vegetables are tender. Sprinkle with cheese. Yield: 8 servings (serving size: 1½ cups soup and 1 tablespoon cheese).

CALORIES 212 (21% from fat); FAT 5g (sat 1.6g, mono 1g, poly 1.2g); PROTEIN 9.6g; CARB 36g; FIBER 3.9g; CHOL 5mg; IRON 1.9mg; SODIUM 961mg; CALC 164mg

Quick Tip: Broiling several quesadillas together on a baking sheet is much faster than cooking them individually in a skillet.

Canadian Cheese Soup with Pumpernickel Croutons

Total time: 35 minutes

- 3 (1-ounce) slices pumpernickel bread, cut into ½-inch cubes
- 1 onion, peeled and quartered
- 1 carrot, peeled and quartered
- 1 celery stalk, quartered
- 1 teaspoon butter
- ¾ cup all-purpose flour
- 2 (14-ounce) cans fat-free, less-sodium chicken broth, divided
- 3 cups 2% reduced-fat milk
- ½ teaspoon salt
- ½ teaspoon paprika
- ½ teaspoon freshly ground black pepper
- 1 ½ cups (6 ounces) shredded reduced-fat sharp cheddar cheese

1. Preheat oven to 375°.

2. Place bread cubes on a jelly-roll pan, and bake at 375° for 15 minutes or until toasted.

3. Combine onion, carrot, and celery in a food processor, and pulse until chopped. Melt butter in a saucepan over medium-high heat. Add vegetables; sauté 5 minutes or until tender.

4. Lightly spoon flour into a dry measuring cup; level with a knife. Gradually add 1 can of broth to flour in a medium bowl; stir well with a whisk. Add flour mixture to vegetable mixture in pan. Stir in 1 can of chicken broth; bring to a boil. Reduce heat to medium, and cook 10 minutes or until thick. Stir in milk, salt, paprika, and pepper; cook for 10 minutes. Remove from heat. Add cheese, and stir until cheese melts. Ladle soup into bowls, and top with croutons. Yield: 8 servings (serving size: 1 cup soup and ¼ cup croutons).

CALORIES 203 (30% from fat); FAT 6.8g (sat 3.8g, mono 1.9g, poly 0.4g); PROTEIN 13.2g; CARB 21.9g; FIBER 1.8g; CHOL 23mg; IRON 1.1mg; SODIUM 671mg; CALC 318mg

Menu   SERVES 8

Canadian Cheese Soup with Pumpernickel Croutons

Tomato salad
Combine 4 cups chopped plum tomatoes, ⅔ cup finely chopped red onion, ⅓ cup fresh lime juice, 2 tablespoons chopped fresh cilantro, 2 tablespoons chopped seeded jalapeño pepper, and ½ teaspoon salt.

Green and red grapes

Game Plan

1 While oven heats for croutons:
- Chop and measure ingredients for soup

2 While croutons bake:
- Prepare soup

3 While soup simmers:
- Prepare salad

Quick Tip: You can make the croutons in advance; let cool and store in an airtight container.

Main Dish

Salads

Let a fresh, colorful, and satisfying salad be the star of your next lunch or dinner.

Menu

SERVES 4

Chicken-Penne Salad with Green Beans

Sesame-garlic braid

Unroll 1 (11-ounce) can refrigerated French bread dough on a baking sheet coated with cooking spray; cut into thirds lengthwise. Braid portions together; pinch loose ends to seal. Combine 2 tablespoons melted butter and 1 teaspoon bottled minced garlic; brush over braid. Sprinkle with 1 tablespoon sesame seeds. Bake at 350° for 25 minutes or until loaf sounds hollow when tapped.

Mixed berries dolloped with vanilla yogurt

Game Plan

1 While water for pasta comes to a boil and oven heats for braid:
- Prepare braid
- Trim and cut green beans
- Shred chicken

2 While pasta and beans cook:
- Slice onion and bell pepper
- Chop basil and parsley
- Prepare dressing
- Prepare berries

Quick Tip:

The texture of shredded chicken allows it to hold the dressing more easily than chicken pieces.

Chicken-Penne Salad with Green Beans

To prepare the beans quickly, trim just the stem ends, leaving the tapered blossom ends intact. Line up five or six beans at a time, and cut them roughly the same length as the pasta.

Total time: 40 minutes

- 2 cups uncooked penne (tube-shaped) pasta
- 2 cups (1-inch) cut green beans (about ½ pound)
- 2 cups shredded cooked chicken breast
- ½ cup vertically sliced red onion
- ¼ cup chopped fresh basil
- 1½ teaspoons chopped fresh flat-leaf parsley
- 1 (7-ounce) bottle roasted red bell peppers, drained and cut into thin strips
- 2 tablespoons extravirgin olive oil
- 2 tablespoons red wine vinegar
- 1 tablespoon cold water
- ½ teaspoon salt
- ¼ teaspoon black pepper
- 1 garlic clove, minced

1. Cook pasta in boiling water 7 minutes. Add green beans; cook 4 minutes. Drain and rinse with cold water; drain.

2. Combine pasta mixture, chicken, onion, basil, parsley, and bell peppers in a large bowl, tossing gently to combine.

3. Combine oil and remaining ingredients in a small bowl, stirring with a whisk. Drizzle over pasta mixture; toss gently to coat. Yield: 4 servings (serving size: 2 cups).

CALORIES 384 (23% from fat); FAT 9.7g (sat 1.8g, mono 5.7g, poly 1.5g); PROTEIN 26.9g; CARB 47.8g; FIBER 2.6g; CHOL 49mg; IRON 3.2mg; SODIUM 866mg; CALC 59mg

Menu

Greek Salad with Grilled Chicken

Oregano breadsticks

Unroll 1 (11-ounce) can refrigerated breadstick dough. Brush dough evenly with 1 tablespoon olive oil; sprinkle with 1 teaspoon dried oregano. Separate dough into individual breadsticks. Place dough sticks on a baking sheet coated with cooking spray. Bake at 375° for 13 minutes or until lightly browned.

Lime sherbet

Game Plan

1 While oven heats for breadsticks:
  • Prepare salad dressing
  • Prepare ingredients for salad

2 Prepare breadsticks and bake.

3 While breadsticks bake:
  • Cook chicken

Quick Tip: Buy packaged, prewashed hearts of romaine lettuce to save time.

Greek Salad with Grilled Chicken

Adding slices of grilled chicken turns the classic Greek salad into a satisfying supper.

Total time: 30 minutes

 ¼ cup fat-free, less-sodium chicken broth
 2 tablespoons red wine vinegar
 1 teaspoon sugar
 1 teaspoon dried oregano
 2 teaspoons olive oil
 ½ teaspoon salt
 ½ teaspoon freshly ground black pepper
 1 garlic clove, minced
 1 pound skinless, boneless chicken breast
Cooking spray
 8 cups torn romaine lettuce
 1 cup sliced cucumber (about 1 small)
 8 pitted kalamata olives, halved
 4 plum tomatoes, quartered lengthwise
 2 (¼-inch-thick) slices red onion, separated into rings
 ¼ cup (1 ounce) crumbled feta cheese

1. Prepare grill or broiler.

2. Combine first 8 ingredients in a large bowl. Brush the chicken with 2 tablespoons dressing.

3. Place chicken on a grill rack or broiler pan coated with cooking spray; cook 5 minutes on each side or until chicken is done. Cut into ¼-inch-thick slices.

4. Add lettuce and next 4 ingredients (through onion) to remaining dressing in large bowl; toss well.

5. Divide salad evenly among 4 plates; top each serving with chicken and cheese. Yield: 4 servings (serving size: 2 cups salad, 3 ounces chicken, and 1 tablespoon cheese).

CALORIES 231 (30% from fat); FAT 7.7g (sat 2.1g, mono 3.9g, poly 1g); PROTEIN 30.3g; CARB 10.3g; FIBER 3.4g; CHOL 72mg; IRON 2.9mg; SODIUM 613mg; CALC 110mg

Grilled Steak Salad with Caper Vinaigrette

This salad is great with leftover beef. If watercress is unavailable, use mixed salad greens. Substitute artichoke hearts for the hearts of palm, or just omit them.

Total time: 40 minutes

SALAD:

1 pound beef tenderloin, trimmed
Cooking spray
4 cups water
3 cups (1-inch) cut green beans (about ½ pound)
4 cups trimmed watercress (about 1 bunch)
1 cup grape tomatoes, halved
¾ cup thinly sliced red onion
1 (8-ounce) package presliced mushrooms
1 (7.75-ounce) can hearts of palm, rinsed and drained

DRESSING:

¼ cup red wine vinegar
1½ tablespoons fresh lemon juice
1 tablespoon capers
1 tablespoon honey mustard
2 teaspoons extravirgin olive oil
½ teaspoon sugar
½ teaspoon salt
⅛ teaspoon freshly ground black pepper

1. Prepare grill or broiler.
2. To prepare salad, place beef on grill rack or broiler pan coated with cooking spray; grill 7 minutes on each side or until desired degree of doneness. Let stand 10 minutes. Cut steak diagonally across grain into thin slices. Place beef in a large bowl.
3. Bring water to a boil in a saucepan; add beans. Cover and cook 3 minutes or until crisp-tender. Rinse with cold water; drain well. Add beans, watercress, tomatoes, onion, mushrooms, and hearts of palm to beef; toss gently to combine.
4. To prepare dressing, combine vinegar, lemon juice, capers, honey mustard, olive oil, sugar, salt, and black pepper, stirring well with a whisk. Drizzle dressing over salad, and toss gently to coat. Yield: 4 servings (serving size: 2 cups).

CALORIES 224 (29% from fat); FAT 7.3g (sat 2g, mono 3.3g, poly 0.5g); PROTEIN 27.3g; CARB 16.8g; FIBER 5.2g; CHOL 60mg; IRON 5.7mg; SODIUM 699mg; CALC 114mg

Menu   SERVES 4

Grilled Steak Salad with Caper Vinaigrette

Mozzarella and basil toast
Place 2 (4-inch) Italian cheese-flavored pizza crusts (such as Boboli) on a baking sheet; top each with ¼ cup shredded part-skim mozzarella cheese and ¼ cup chopped fresh basil. Bake at 425° for 8 minutes or until cheese melts. Cut each crust into quarters.

Fresh fruit

Game Plan

1 While grill or broiler heats:
  • Cook green beans
  • Combine salad ingredients
  • Prepare dressing

2 While beef cooks:
  • Prepare toast

3 Toss salad.

Quick Tip: Sliced roast beef from the deli counter can cut your prep time in half.

Menu

Chicken Salad with Nectarines in Mint Vinaigrette

....

Peppery cheese breadsticks

Combine ½ cup grated Romano cheese and 1 tablespoon freshly ground black pepper in a shallow dish. Unroll 1 (11-ounce) can refrigerated soft breadsticks; separate into 12 portions. Roll each dough portion in cheese mixture, turning and pressing gently to coat. Twist each dough portion gently; place on a baking sheet coated with cooking spray. Bake at 375° for 13 minutes or until golden brown.

....

Lemonade

....

Game Plan

1 While oven heats:
 • Prepare dressing
 • Prepare breadsticks

2 While breadsticks bake:
 • Prepare and toss salad

Chicken Salad with Nectarines in Mint Vinaigrette

The mint adds a refreshing note to the dressing, which would also work well in a fresh fruit salad. Use any curly lettuce leaves in place of red leaf.

Total time: 22 minutes

DRESSING:

 1 cup loosely packed fresh mint leaves
 ⅓ cup sugar
 ¼ cup white wine vinegar
 1 tablespoon fresh lemon juice
 ¼ teaspoon salt
 ¼ teaspoon freshly ground black pepper

SALAD:

 2 cups chopped cooked chicken breast
 1 cup chopped seeded cucumber
 ⅓ cup chopped pecans, toasted
 2 tablespoons minced red onion
 3 nectarines, chopped, peeled, and pitted
 5 red leaf lettuce leaves

1. To prepare dressing, place mint and sugar in a food processor; process until finely chopped, scraping sides of the bowl. Add vinegar, lemon juice, salt, and black pepper; process 30 seconds to combine.

2. To prepare salad, combine chicken, cucumber, pecans, onion, and nectarines in a medium bowl. Drizzle dressing over salad; toss well to coat. Place 1 lettuce leaf on each of 5 plates; top each serving with ¾ cup salad. Yield: 5 servings.

CALORIES 241 (28% from fat); FAT 7.4g (sat 1g, mono 3.6g, poly 2.1g); PROTEIN 16.7g; CARB 29g; FIBER 3.6g; CHOL 39mg; IRON 3.4mg; SODIUM 163mg; CALC 71mg

Quick Tip: In a pinch, substitute fresh melon for the nectarines. Look for chopped peeled melon in the produce section at the supermarket.

Thai Beef Salad

The salad gets its heat from two tablespoons of chile paste. If you prefer milder food, use half the amount. Fresh mint adds a cooling contrast.

Total time: 42 minutes

½ cup fresh lime juice (about 4 limes)
¼ cup chopped fresh cilantro
2 tablespoons brown sugar
2 tablespoons Thai fish sauce
2 tablespoons chile paste with garlic
2 garlic cloves, minced
1 (1½-pound) flank steak, trimmed
Cooking spray
1½ cups vertically sliced red onion
4 plum tomatoes, each cut into 6 wedges
1¼ cups thinly sliced English cucumber
2 tablespoons chopped fresh mint
1 (10-ounce) package torn romaine lettuce (about 6 cups)

1. Prepare grill or broiler.

2. Combine first 6 ingredients, stirring until sugar dissolves; set half of lime mixture aside. Combine the other half of lime mixture and steak in a large zip-top plastic bag; seal. Marinate in refrigerator 10 minutes, turning once. Remove steak from bag, and discard marinade.

3. Place steak on grill rack or broiler pan coated with cooking spray; cook 6 minutes on each side or until desired degree of doneness. Let stand 5 minutes. Cut steak diagonally across grain into thin slices.

4. Heat a large nonstick skillet over medium-high heat. Coat pan with cooking spray. Add onion, and sauté 3 minutes. Add tomatoes; sauté 2 minutes. Place onion mixture, cucumber, mint, and lettuce in a large bowl; toss gently to combine. Divide the salad evenly among 6 plates. Top each serving with 3 ounces steak; drizzle each serving with 1 tablespoon reserved lime mixture. Yield: 6 servings.

CALORIES 219 (35% from fat); FAT 8.6g (sat 3.6g, mono 3.3g, poly 0.5g); PROTEIN 24.1g; CARB 12.3g; FIBER 2.2g; CHOL 54mg; IRON 3.1mg; SODIUM 456mg; CALC 44mg

Menu   SERVES 6

Thai Beef Salad

Coconut rice

Bring ½ cup water, ¼ teaspoon salt, and 1 (14-ounce) can light coconut milk to a simmer in a medium saucepan. Add 1 cup jasmine rice; cover and simmer 20 minutes or until liquid is absorbed. Remove from heat; let stand 5 minutes. Fluff with a fork.

Strawberry sorbet

Game Plan

1 While water for rice comes to a boil:
• Prepare marinade; marinate steak

2 While rice cooks:
• Slice onion
• Cut tomatoes into wedges
• Cook steak
• Prepare lettuce, cucumber, and mint for the salad

Quick Tip: English cucumbers work well for quick meals because they're virtually seedless.

Menu   SERVES 4

**Grilled Jamaican Pork
Tenderloin Salad**

Roasted sweet potato wedges
*Combine 2 pounds sweet potato, cut into
¹⁄₂-inch wedges, 2 tablespoons vegetable oil,
¹⁄₂ teaspoon salt, and ¹⁄₈ teaspoon ground
red pepper in a large bowl; toss to coat.
Arrange wedges on a baking sheet; bake at
425° for 25 minutes or until tender and
lightly browned, turning occasionally.*

**Hummus with sesame
breadsticks**

Game Plan

1 While grill heats for pork and oven
heats for potatoes:
  • Prepare dressing
  • Prepare pork
  • Prepare sweet potatoes

2 While pork and potatoes cook:
  • Prepare salad

Quick Tip: Look for cored fresh
pineapple in the produce section at
the grocery store. You also can buy
bottled sliced papaya.

Grilled Jamaican Pork Tenderloin Salad

Butterflying the pork helps it cook faster. If you can't find papaya, use an extra cup of
chopped pineapple.

Total time: 34 minutes

DRESSING:
  2 tablespoons fresh or 2 teaspoons
     dried thyme leaves
  2 tablespoons fresh lime juice
  1 tablespoon olive oil
  1 tablespoon minced fresh
     ginger
  2 teaspoons brown sugar
  ¹⁄₂ teaspoon salt
  ¹⁄₂ teaspoon ground allspice
  ¹⁄₂ teaspoon ground cinnamon
  ¹⁄₄ teaspoon freshly ground black
     pepper
  ¹⁄₄ teaspoon ground nutmeg
  1 garlic clove, minced

SALAD:
  1 (1-pound) pork tenderloin
  Cooking spray
  4 cups mixed salad greens
  2 cups chopped peeled fresh
     pineapple
  1 cup chopped peeled papaya

1. Prepare grill or broiler.
2. To prepare dressing, combine first
11 ingredients in a food processor;
process until smooth.
3. To prepare pork, slice pork lengthwise, cutting to, but not through,
other side. Open halves, laying pork
flat. Rub 2 tablespoons dressing on
pork, and reserve remaining dressing.
Place pork on grill rack or broiler pan
coated with cooking spray; cook 10
minutes on each side or until a meat
thermometer registers 155°. Let pork
stand 5 minutes. Cut pork into ¹⁄₄-
inch-thick slices, and toss with reserved dressing.
4. Place 1 cup salad greens on each of
4 plates; top with 3 ounces pork, ¹⁄₂
cup pineapple, and ¹⁄₄ cup papaya.
Yield: 4 servings.

CALORIES 263 (30% from fat); FAT 8.7g (sat 2.3g, mono 4.8g, poly
0.9g); PROTEIN 28.4g; CARB 18.3g; FIBER 3.2g; CHOL 69mg; IRON
2.7mg; SODIUM 371mg; CALC 78mg

Chicken, Red Potato, and Green Bean Salad

Red potatoes work well and add a nice color to this salad, but you can use any waxy potato, such as fingerling or white. If your potatoes aren't about golf ball–sized, cut each into eight wedges before beginning to cook.

Total time: 35 minutes

DRESSING:
- ⅓ cup coarsely chopped fresh parsley
- 3 tablespoons red wine vinegar
- 1 tablespoon fresh lemon juice
- 1 tablespoon whole-grain Dijon mustard
- 1 tablespoon extravirgin olive oil
- ½ teaspoon salt
- ¼ teaspoon freshly ground black pepper
- 1 garlic clove, minced

SALAD:
- 1 pound small red potatoes
- 1 teaspoon salt
- ½ pound diagonally cut green beans
- 2 cups cubed cooked chicken (about 8 ounces)
- 2 tablespoons chopped red onion
- 1 (10-ounce) package gourmet salad greens (about 6 cups)

1. To prepare dressing, combine first 8 ingredients, stirring well with a whisk.

2. To prepare salad, place potatoes in a saucepan; cover with water. Add 1 teaspoon salt to pan; bring to a boil. Reduce heat; simmer 10 minutes or until almost tender. Add beans; cook 4 minutes or until crisp-tender. Drain. Rinse with cold water; drain well.

3. Quarter potatoes. Place potatoes, beans, chicken, onion, and greens in a large bowl. Drizzle with dressing; toss gently to coat. Serve immediately. Yield: 4 servings (serving size: about 1¾ cups).

CALORIES 269 (29% from fat); FAT 8.8g (sat 1.8g, mono 4.4g, poly 1.6g); PROTEIN 22.4g; CARB 26.1g; FIBER 5.8g; CHOL 53mg; IRON 3.8mg; SODIUM 761mg; CALC 96mg

Quick Tip: Use a roasted whole chicken purchased from the deli at your supermarket, and you'll have leftovers for another meal.

Menu   SERVES 4

Chicken, Red Potato, and Green Bean Salad

Garlic-Parmesan toasts
Combine 2 tablespoons grated fresh Parmesan cheese, 2 tablespoons softened butter, ¼ teaspoon salt, ⅛ teaspoon freshly ground black pepper, and 1 minced garlic clove in a small bowl, stirring well. Spread butter mixture evenly over 8 (1-ounce) French bread baguette slices. Bake at 425° for 6 minutes or until golden brown.

Sliced plum tomatoes

Game Plan

1 While potatoes and green beans cook:
- Preheat oven
- Prepare dressing
- Chop chicken and onion
- Prepare ingredients for Parmesan toasts

2 While toasts cook:
- Slice tomatoes
- Combine salad

Menu

Chicken and Couscous Salad

Pita crisps

Split 1 pita in half horizontally; cut each half into 6 wedges. Place wedges in a single layer on a baking sheet. Lightly coat with cooking spray; sprinkle with ⅛ teaspoon salt and ⅛ teaspoon freshly ground black pepper. Bake at 350° for 15 minutes or until crisp and golden brown.

Lemon sorbet

Game Plan

1 While oven heats:
- Prepare couscous
- Prepare dressing
- Season pita wedges

2 While pita wedges bake:
- Prepare salad

Quick Tip: You can toast nuts quickly in a dry skillet over medium-high heat. Stir frequently, and as soon as they become fragrant, remove the nuts from the pan.

Chicken and Couscous Salad

If you can't find the specified box size of couscous, you can use one cup uncooked couscous. If you have any salad left, take it to work for a light lunch.

Total time: 25 minutes

SALAD:
1¼ cups fat-free, less-sodium chicken broth
1 (5.7-ounce) box uncooked couscous
1½ cups cubed cooked chicken (about 6 ounces)
½ cup thinly sliced green onions
½ cup diced radishes (about 3 large)
½ cup chopped seeded peeled cucumber
¼ cup chopped fresh flat-leaf parsley
2 tablespoons pine nuts, toasted

DRESSING:
¼ cup white wine vinegar
1½ tablespoons extravirgin olive oil
1 teaspoon ground cumin
½ teaspoon salt
⅛ teaspoon freshly ground black pepper
1 garlic clove, minced

1. To prepare salad, bring broth to a boil in a medium saucepan; gradually stir in couscous. Remove from heat; cover and let stand 5 minutes. Fluff with a fork. Spoon couscous into a large bowl; cool slightly. Add chicken, onions, radishes, cucumber, parsley, and pine nuts; toss gently to combine.

2. To prepare dressing, combine vinegar and remaining ingredients, stirring with a whisk. Drizzle dressing over salad; toss to combine. Yield: 4 servings (serving size: 1½ cups).

CALORIES 334 (29% from fat); FAT 10.9g (sat 2g, mono 5.9g, poly 2.1g); PROTEIN 20.9g; CARB 35.8g; FIBER 2.9g; CHOL 39mg; IRON 1.8mg; SODIUM 484mg; CALC 23mg

Mediterranean Salad with Shrimp

Use shredded rotisserie chicken in place of the shrimp, if you'd prefer.

Total time: 25 minutes

- 4 quarts water
- 1½ pounds large shrimp, peeled and deveined
- 1½ cups halved cherry tomatoes
- 1 cup (¼-inch-thick) slices red onion, separated into rings
- 1 cup (¼-inch-thick) slices cucumber, halved
- 1 (10-ounce) package torn romaine lettuce (about 6 cups)
- 1 tablespoon chopped fresh flat-leaf parsley
- 3 tablespoons red wine vinegar
- 2 teaspoons Dijon mustard
- 1 teaspoon extravirgin olive oil
- ¾ teaspoon dried oregano
- ¼ teaspoon salt
- ¼ teaspoon black pepper
- 2 garlic cloves, minced
- ½ cup (2 ounces) crumbled feta cheese
- 8 kalamata olives, pitted and halved
- 4 pepperoncini peppers

1. Bring water to a boil in a large saucepan. Add shrimp; cook 2 minutes or until done. Drain and rinse with cold water. Place shrimp in a bowl; cover and chill.

2. Place tomatoes, onion, cucumber, and lettuce in a large bowl; toss to combine. Combine parsley and next 7 ingredients (through garlic), stirring with a whisk. Spoon 1 tablespoon of dressing over shrimp; toss to combine. Add shrimp mixture and remaining dressing to lettuce mixture, and toss gently to coat.

3. Spoon about 2¾ cups salad onto each of 4 plates. Top each serving with 2 tablespoons cheese, 4 olive halves, and 1 pepperoncini pepper. Yield: 4 servings.

CALORIES 296 (30% from fat); FAT 9.8g (sat 3.2g, mono 3.6g, poly 1.8g); PROTEIN 39.4g; CARB 12.1g; FIBER 3.2g; CHOL 271mg; IRON 6mg; SODIUM 849mg; CALC 219mg

Quick Tip: For quick suppers, keep a bag of cooked, peeled, and deveined shrimp in the freezer. Set the shrimp in a colander and rinse with cool water to thaw quickly.

Menu   SERVES 4

Mediterranean Salad with Shrimp

Oregano pita crisps
Cut each of 2 (6-inch) pitas into 8 wedges; arrange pita wedges in a single layer on a baking sheet. Lightly coat pita wedges with cooking spray. Combine ½ teaspoon dried oregano, ⅛ teaspoon salt, ⅛ teaspoon garlic powder, and ⅛ teaspoon black pepper; sprinkle evenly over pita wedges. Lightly coat pita wedges again with cooking spray. Bake at 400° for 10 minutes or until golden.

Vanilla low-fat yogurt topped with honey and sliced almonds

Game Plan

1 While oven heats for pita crisps and water for shrimp comes to a boil:
- Peel and devein shrimp
- Prepare lettuce mixture
- Prepare herb mixture for pita crisps

2 While pita crisps bake:
- Cook shrimp
- Crumble feta cheese
- Pit and halve olives

Menu

SERVES 6

Summer Farfalle Salad with Smoked Salmon

Artichoke-Parmesan cream cheese with crackers

Combine ¾ cup tub-style light cream cheese, ¼ cup chopped canned artichoke hearts, 3 tablespoons grated Parmesan cheese, and ¼ teaspoon garlic salt. Serve with crackers.

Sliced peaches

Game Plan

1 While water for pasta comes to a boil:
- Halve cherry tomatoes
- Chop dill
- Prepare artichoke-Parmesan cream cheese

2 While pasta cooks:
- Prepare dressing for salad
- Cut salmon
- Slice peaches

Summer Farfalle Salad with Smoked Salmon

Total time: 35 minutes

  3 cups uncooked farfalle (bow tie pasta)
  2 cups cherry tomatoes, halved
  ¼ cup chopped fresh dill
  1 (6-ounce) package fresh baby spinach
  1 teaspoon grated lemon rind
  2 tablespoons fresh lemon juice
  2 tablespoons cold water
1½ tablespoons extravirgin olive oil
  ½ teaspoon salt
  ¼ teaspoon black pepper
  4 ounces (about 8 slices) smoked salmon, cut into thin strips

1. Cook pasta according to package directions, omitting salt and fat. Drain and rinse with cold water; drain.

2. Combine pasta, tomatoes, dill, and spinach in a large bowl, tossing gently to combine.

3. Combine lemon rind and next 5 ingredients (through pepper) in a small bowl, stirring with a whisk. Drizzle over pasta mixture; toss gently to coat. Top with salmon. Yield: 6 servings (serving size: 2 cups).

CALORIES 206 (23% from fat); FAT 5.3g (sat 0.9g, mono 3.1g, poly 1.1g); PROTEIN 9.8g; CARB 31.4g; FIBER 2.7g; CHOL 4mg; IRON 2.3mg; SODIUM 603mg; CALC 43mg

Quick Tip: Look for sliced smoked salmon near the gourmet cheeses or in the seafood department. Freeze leftover salmon for later use—sprinkle on scrambled eggs, or add to a toasted bagel with light cream cheese.

Orzo Salad with Chickpeas, Dill, and Lemon

The bright flavor of this salad pairs well with the crisp romaine-mint side salad. If you're sensitive to dill, use half the amount. Couscous can be substituted for orzo.

Total time: 30 minutes

- 1 cup uncooked orzo (rice-shaped pasta)
- ½ cup thinly sliced green onions
- ½ cup (2 ounces) crumbled feta cheese
- ¼ cup chopped fresh dill
- 1 (19-ounce) can chickpeas (garbanzo beans), drained
- 3 tablespoons fresh lemon juice
- 1½ tablespoons extravirgin olive oil
- 1 tablespoon cold water
- ½ teaspoon salt
- ½ teaspoon bottled minced garlic

1. Cook pasta according to package directions, omitting salt and fat. Drain and rinse with cold water; drain.

2. Combine pasta, onions, feta cheese, dill, and chickpeas in a large bowl, tossing gently to combine.

3. Combine juice and remaining ingredients in a small bowl, stirring with a whisk. Drizzle over pasta mixture; toss gently to coat. Yield: 4 servings (serving size: 1¼ cups).

CALORIES 327 (29% from fat); FAT 10.4g (sat 2.9g, mono 5.1g, poly 1.8g); PROTEIN 10.8g; CARB 47.6g; FIBER 4.9g; CHOL 13mg; IRON 3mg; SODIUM 641mg; CALC 107mg

Quick Tip: To get more juice from a lemon, be sure it's at room temperature. Then, before juicing, roll it across the countertop while applying pressure with the palm of your hand.

Menu
SERVES 4

Orzo Salad with Chickpeas, Dill, and Lemon

Chopped romaine with mint
Combine 4 cups thinly sliced romaine lettuce and ½ cup chopped fresh mint in a bowl. Combine 1 tablespoon fresh lemon juice, 2 teaspoons olive oil, and ⅛ teaspoon salt in a small bowl, stirring with a whisk. Drizzle over salad; toss to combine.

Garlic breadsticks

Game Plan

1 While water for pasta comes to a boil and oven heats for breadsticks:
- Slice green onions
- Chop dill
- Drain chickpeas

2 While pasta cooks:
- Bake breadsticks
- Prepare romaine salad
- Prepare dressing for orzo salad

Meatless

Only minutes in the making, these meatless menus creatively marry fresh ingredients.

PHOTOGRAPHY: BECKY LUIGART-STAYNER/STYLING: CINDY BARR

Menu

Red Bell Pepper Frittata

Toasted bagels with cream cheese and strawberry jam

Roasted apples
Combine 2 cups sliced Granny Smith apples, 1 ½ tablespoons maple syrup, and 1 teaspoon melted butter in an 8-inch square baking dish coated with cooking spray. Bake at 400° for 15 minutes or until tender.

Game Plan

1 While oven heats for apples and the water for couscous comes to a boil:
  - Slice onion and bell pepper
  - Mince garlic
  - Combine egg mixture

2 While apples roast and couscous stands:
  - Toast bagels
  - Start to cook frittata

Quick Tip:
Look for packaged sliced Granny Smith apples in the produce section.

Red Bell Pepper Frittata

Cooked couscous makes this meatless entrée more filling. Substitute one cup leftover cooked spaghetti or vermicelli, if you prefer.

Total time: 30 minutes

½ cup water	2 cups red bell pepper strips
⅓ cup uncooked couscous	1 cup thinly vertically sliced onion
1 tablespoon water	2 garlic cloves, minced
¾ teaspoon salt	⅓ cup (about 1½ ounces) shredded Manchego cheese or Monterey Jack cheese
¼ teaspoon black pepper	
4 large egg whites	
3 large eggs	
Cooking spray	

1. Preheat oven to 350°.

2. Bring ½ cup water to a boil in a small saucepan; gradually stir in couscous. Remove from heat; cover and let stand 5 minutes. Fluff with a fork.

3. Combine 1 tablespoon water, salt, black pepper, egg whites, and eggs in a medium bowl, stirring with a whisk.

4. Heat a 10-inch ovenproof nonstick skillet over medium-high heat. Coat pan with cooking spray. Add bell pepper, onion, and garlic; sauté 5 minutes. Stir in couscous and egg mixture; cook over medium heat 5 minutes or until almost set. Sprinkle with cheese. Bake at 350° for 10 minutes or until set. Let stand 5 minutes before serving. Yield: 4 servings (serving size: 1 wedge).

CALORIES 204 (30% from fat); FAT 6.8g (sat 3g, mono 2.3g, poly 0.7g); PROTEIN 15g; CARB 20.6g; FIBER 2.9g; CHOL 167mg; IRON 1.3mg; SODIUM 716mg; CALC 169mg

meatless

Menu

SERVES 4

Curried Noodles with Tofu

Sesame-scented snow peas and carrots

Cook 1½ cups snow peas and ½ cup diagonally sliced carrot in boiling water 30 seconds; drain. Toss vegetables with 2 teaspoons low-sodium soy sauce, 1 teaspoon dark sesame oil, 1 teaspoon rice vinegar, and ½ teaspoon sugar.

Green tea

Game Plan

1 While water comes to a boil for snow peas and carrots:
- Prepare tofu, red bell pepper, cabbage, green onions, and cilantro
- Combine sauce ingredients

2 While tofu is sautéing:
- Soak rice sticks in hot water

3 While noodle mixture cooks:
- Toss snow peas and carrots with seasonings

Curried Noodles with Tofu

Coconut milk gives this meatless dish a velvety richness. Look for green curry paste in the Asian foods section. Use it conservatively, though—a little goes a long way.

Total time: 33 minutes

- 6 ounces uncooked rice sticks (rice-flour noodles), angel hair pasta, or vermicelli
- 1 cup light coconut milk
- 1 tablespoon sugar
- 2 tablespoons low-sodium soy sauce
- 1½ tablespoons grated peeled fresh ginger
- 1 teaspoon green curry paste
- ½ teaspoon salt
- 4 garlic cloves, minced
- Cooking spray
- 1 (12.3-ounce) package extrafirm tofu, drained and cut into 1-inch cubes
- 1 cup red bell pepper strips
- 4 cups shredded napa (Chinese) cabbage
- 1 cup chopped green onions
- 3 tablespoons chopped fresh cilantro

1. Place noodles in a large bowl. Add hot water to cover; let stand 5 minutes. Drain.

2. Combine light coconut milk, sugar, low-sodium soy sauce, fresh ginger, green curry paste, salt, and minced garlic in a small bowl.

3. Heat a large nonstick skillet over medium-high heat. Coat pan with cooking spray. Add tofu; sauté 10 minutes or until golden brown. Remove tofu from pan; keep warm.

4. Add bell pepper to pan; sauté 1 minute or until crisp-tender. Add cabbage; sauté 30 seconds. Stir in noodles, coconut milk mixture, and tofu; cook 2 minutes or until noodles are tender. Stir in green onions and fresh cilantro. Yield: 4 servings (serving size: 1¼ cups).

CALORIES 300 (15% from fat); FAT 4.9g (sat 2.3g, mono 0.4g, poly 1.1g); PROTEIN 11.5g; CARB 51.4g; FIBER 4.5g; CHOL 0mg; IRON 3.6mg; SODIUM 678mg; CALC 89mg

Quick Tip: You can use the hot water left over from cooking the snow peas and carrots to soak the rice sticks. Remove the vegetables with a slotted spoon, and pour the cooking water over the noodles.

Onion Bread Pudding

Although the nutty flavor of Gruyère cheese pairs nicely with the sweet onion, Parmesan, fontina, or Monterey Jack would also work well in this recipe.

Total time: 40 minutes

- 1 Vidalia or other sweet onion, cut into ¼-inch-thick slices
- 2 cups 2% reduced-fat milk
- ½ teaspoon salt
- ½ teaspoon dried thyme
- ⅛ teaspoon freshly ground black pepper
- 2 large eggs, lightly beaten
- 8 cups cubed French bread (about 8 ounces)
- ¾ cup (3 ounces) shredded Gruyère or Swiss cheese, divided

Cooking spray

1. Preheat oven to 425°.

2. Heat a large nonstick skillet over medium-high heat. Add onion slices (keep slices intact); cook 3 minutes on each side or until browned.

3. Combine milk, salt, thyme, pepper, and eggs in a large bowl, stirring with a whisk. Add bread cubes and ½ cup cheese; toss well. Place the bread mixture in an 8-inch square baking dish coated with cooking spray. Arrange onion slices on top of bread mixture. Sprinkle with ¼ cup cheese. Bake at 425° for 25 minutes or until set and golden. Yield: 4 servings (serving size: about 1½ cups).

CALORIES 364 (30% from fat); FAT 12.2g (sat 5.7g, mono 3.7g, poly 1.1g); PROTEIN 19.7g; CARB 43.8g; FIBER 3.4g; CHOL 136mg; IRON 2.1mg; SODIUM 806mg; CALC 294mg

Menu   SERVES 4

Onion Bread Pudding

Asparagus salad
Combine 4 cups (½-inch) cooked asparagus pieces, 1 cup chopped plum tomato, ¼ cup chopped red onion, ¼ cup crumbled feta cheese, 2 tablespoons fresh lemon juice, 2 teaspoons chopped fresh dill, 1 teaspoon olive oil, and ¼ teaspoon salt, stirring well.

Fresh fruit

Game Plan

1 While oven heats:
- Cook onion slices
- Prepare bread and milk mixture

2 While bread pudding bakes:
- Prepare asparagus salad

Quick Tip: You can assemble the bread pudding ahead of time; cover and refrigerate until you're ready to bake it.

Menu

SERVES 4

Huevos Rancheros with Queso Fresco

....

Orange, pineapple, and coconut ambrosia

Drain 1 (15¼-ounce) can pineapple chunks in juice and 1 (14-ounce) jar fresh orange sections. Combine pineapple, orange, and 2 tablespoons powdered sugar, tossing to coat. Sprinkle with ⅓ cup flaked sweetened coconut.

....

Margaritas

....

Game Plan

1 Prepare ambrosia; cover and chill until serving time.

2 While tomato mixture cooks:
 • Chop cilantro
 • Squeeze lime juice
 • Heat beans

3 While eggs cook:
 • Heat tortillas
 • Prepare margaritas

Quick Tip: Corn tortillas are often used in this dish. You can use them, if you have some on hand.

Huevos Rancheros with Queso Fresco

Queso fresco is a soft, crumbly, salty Mexican cheese. Look for it in cottage cheese–style tubs in the dairy section of large grocery stores and Hispanic markets. Substitute crumbled feta or goat cheese, if you prefer.

Total time: 25 minutes

 1 (10-ounce) can diced tomatoes and green chiles, undrained
 1 (10-ounce) can red enchilada sauce
 ⅓ cup chopped fresh cilantro
 1 tablespoon fresh lime juice
 2 tablespoons water
 1 (16-ounce) can pinto beans, rinsed and drained
 Cooking spray
 4 large eggs
 4 (8-inch) fat-free flour tortillas
 1 cup (4 ounces) crumbled queso fresco

1. Combine tomatoes and enchilada sauce in a medium saucepan; bring to a boil. Reduce heat; simmer, uncovered, for 5 minutes or until slightly thick. Remove from heat; stir in cilantro and juice, and set aside.

2. Place water and pinto beans in a microwave-safe bowl, and partially mash with a fork. Cover and microwave at HIGH 2 minutes or until hot.

3. Heat a large nonstick skillet over medium-high heat. Coat pan with cooking spray. Add eggs, and cook 1 minute on each side or until desired degree of doneness.

4. Warm tortillas according to package directions. Spread about ⅓ cup beans over each tortilla; top each tortilla with 1 egg. Spoon ½ cup sauce around each egg; sprinkle each serving with ¼ cup cheese. Yield: 4 servings (serving size: 1 topped tortilla).

CALORIES 340 (26% from fat); FAT 9.8g (sat 3.2g, mono 2.7g, poly 1g); PROTEIN 15.7g; CARB 37.8g; FIBER 6.1g; CHOL 222mg; IRON 2.1mg; SODIUM 970mg; CALC 153mg

Lasagna Rolls with Roasted Red Pepper Sauce

These rolls require some assembly time but are a nice change of pace from layered pasta. They also make a pretty presentation on a plate.

Total time: 45 minutes

LASAGNA:

- 8 uncooked lasagna noodles
- 4 teaspoons olive oil
- ½ cup finely chopped onion
- 1 (8-ounce) package presliced mushrooms
- 1 (6-ounce) package baby spinach
- 3 garlic cloves, minced
- ½ cup (2 ounces) shredded mozzarella cheese
- ½ cup part-skim ricotta cheese
- ¼ cup minced fresh basil, divided
- ½ teaspoon salt
- ¼ teaspoon crushed red pepper

SAUCE:

- 1 tablespoon red wine vinegar
- ¼ teaspoon salt
- ⅛ teaspoon black pepper
- 2 garlic cloves, minced
- 1 (14.5-ounce) can diced tomatoes
- 1 (7-ounce) bottle roasted red bell peppers, undrained
- ⅛ teaspoon crushed red pepper

1. To prepare lasagna, cook noodles according to the package directions, omitting salt and fat. Drain and rinse noodles under cold water. Drain.

2. Heat oil in a large nonstick skillet over medium-high heat. Add onion, mushrooms, spinach, and 3 garlic cloves; sauté 5 minutes or until onion and mushrooms are tender. Remove from heat; stir in cheeses, 2 tablespoons basil, ½ teaspoon salt, and ¼ teaspoon crushed red pepper.

3. To prepare sauce, place vinegar and the remaining sauce ingredients in a blender; process until smooth.

4. Place cooked noodles on a flat surface; spread ¼ cup cheese mixture over each noodle. Roll up noodles, jelly-roll fashion, starting with short side. Place the rolls, seam sides down, in a shallow 2-quart microwave-safe dish. Pour ¼ cup sauce over each roll, and cover with heavy-duty plastic wrap. Microwave at HIGH 5 minutes or until thoroughly heated. Sprinkle with remaining 2 tablespoons basil. Yield: 4 servings (serving size: 2 rolls).

CALORIES 393 (27% from fat); FAT 11.7g (sat 4.3g, mono 3.6g, poly 1.5g); PROTEIN 19.3g; CARB 58.3g; FIBER 5.9g; CHOL 20mg; IRON 3.8mg; SODIUM 924mg; CALC 253mg

---

Menu
SERVES 4

Lasagna Rolls with Roasted Red Pepper Sauce

Sugar snap peas

Amaretto pears
Cut 2 pears into thin slices. Combine pear slices, 2 tablespoons toasted sliced almonds, 1 tablespoon brown sugar, and 1 tablespoon amaretto.

Game Plan

1 While water comes to a boil:
- Chop onion and garlic
- Shred cheese

2 While noodles cook:
- Prepare sauce
- Prepare pears
- Blanch snap peas

Quick Tip: Use baby spinach to eliminate the task of trimming stems.

Menu

**Rice Noodles with Tofu
and Bok Choy**

....

Asian spinach salad

*Combine 2 cups fresh spinach, 1 cup grated
carrot, and 1 cup bean sprouts in a large
bowl. Combine 1 tablespoon fresh lime juice,
1 tablespoon rice vinegar, 2 teaspoons low-
sodium soy sauce, ½ teaspoon sugar, and
½ teaspoon sesame oil, stirring well with a
whisk. Toss with spinach mixture. Top each
serving with 1 teaspoon chopped dry-
roasted peanuts.*

....

Iced green tea with mint leaves

Game Plan

1 While water comes to a boil:
  • Chop vegetables and tofu

2 While noodles cook:
  • Prepare soy sauce mixture
  • Prepare spinach mixture
  • Prepare salad dressing

3 While tofu mixture cooks:
  • Slice green onions
  • Chop cilantro
  • Toss salad with dressing

Rice Noodles with Tofu and Bok Choy

Look for water-packed tofu, which will hold its shape when cooked and tossed with the
noodles. If rice noodles are unavailable, substitute angel hair pasta.

Total time: 24 minutes

1 (6-ounce) package rice noodles
¼ cup low-sodium soy sauce
2 tablespoons rice vinegar
1 teaspoon sugar
1 teaspoon dark sesame oil
½ teaspoon crushed red pepper
Cooking spray
2 cups (¼-inch-thick) red bell
  pepper strips
5 cups sliced bok choy
½ pound firm water-packed tofu,
  drained and cut into ½-inch
  cubes
3 garlic cloves, minced
½ cup thinly sliced green onions
3 tablespoons chopped fresh
  cilantro

1. Cook noodles in boiling water 6
minutes; drain. Combine soy sauce,
vinegar, sugar, oil, and crushed red
pepper, stirring well with a whisk.

2. Heat a large nonstick skillet over
medium-high heat. Coat pan with
cooking spray. Add bell pepper strips;
sauté 2 minutes. Add bok choy; sauté
1 minute. Add tofu and garlic; sauté 2
minutes. Add noodles and soy sauce
mixture; cook 2 minutes or until thoroughly heated, tossing well to coat.
Sprinkle with sliced green onions and
cilantro. Yield: 4 servings (serving
size: 2 cups).

CALORIES 281 (17% from fat); FAT 5.2g (sat 0.8g, mono 0.9g, poly
2.3g); PROTEIN 12.9g; CARB 46.7g; FIBER 4.2g; CHOL 0mg; IRON
3.8mg; SODIUM 575mg; CALC 190mg

Quick Tip: If you can't find bok choy, almost any quick-cooking
crisp vegetable will work; try shredded Napa cabbage.

Black Bean Burrito Bake

Half of the beans are finely chopped to give the filling a thick, creamy consistency.

Total time: 45 minutes

1   (7-ounce) can chipotle
    chiles in adobo sauce
½   cup reduced-fat sour
    cream
1   (15-ounce) can black beans,
    rinsed, drained, and divided
1   cup frozen whole-kernel corn,
    thawed
4   (8-inch) flour tortillas
Cooking spray
1   cup bottled salsa
½   cup (2 ounces) shredded
    Monterey Jack cheese

1. Preheat oven to 350°.

2. Remove one chile from can. Chop chile. Reserve remaining adobo sauce and chiles for another use. Combine chile and sour cream in a medium bowl; let stand 10 minutes.

3. Place half of beans in a food processor; process until finely chopped. Add chopped beans, remaining beans, and corn to sour cream mixture.

4. Spoon ½ cup bean mixture down center of each tortilla. Roll up tortillas; place, seam sides down, in an 11 x 7–inch baking dish coated with cooking spray. Spread salsa over tortillas; sprinkle with cheese. Cover and bake at 350° for 20 minutes or until thoroughly heated. Yield: 4 servings (serving size: 1 burrito).

CALORIES 365 (29% from fat); FAT 11.7g (sat 5.8g, mono 2.8g, poly 0.8g); PROTEIN 15.7g; CARB 55.3g; FIBER 7.2g; CHOL 28mg; IRON 3.5mg; SODIUM 893mg; CALC 311mg

Quick Tip: This dish can be put together up to eight hours in advance and chilled. Bring to room temperature before baking.

Menu
SERVES 4

Black Bean Burrito Bake
....
Yellow rice
....
Margarita ice cream
Combine 1 pint softened low-fat vanilla ice cream, 2 tablespoons fresh lime juice, 1 tablespoon fresh orange juice, 1 tablespoon tequila, and ⅛ teaspoon salt, stirring well to combine. Freeze to desired consistency.
....

Game Plan

1 While ice cream softens and
   oven heats:
   • Combine adobo sauce and
     sour cream

2 Stir ingredients into ice cream.

3 Prepare burritos.

4 While burritos bake:
   • Prepare rice

Menu

Greek-Style Stuffed Eggplant

....

Herbed goat cheese toasts

Combine ½ cup crumbled goat cheese, ¾ teaspoon dried oregano, ½ teaspoon garlic powder, ¼ teaspoon paprika, and ⅛ teaspoon salt; sprinkle evenly over 8 (1-ounce) slices French bread. Broil 2 minutes or until lightly browned.

....

Lemon sorbet with almond biscotti

....

Game Plan

1 Remove eggplant pulp.

2 While eggplant shells cook:
  • Preheat broiler
  • Slice bread
  • Prepare breadcrumb mixture

3 While eggplant filling cooks:
  • Prepare toasts

4 Broil stuffed eggplant shells.

Quick Tip: To save time or if you don't have leftover French bread to make breadcrumbs, use ½ cup canned dry breadcrumbs.

Greek-Style Stuffed Eggplant

Leave about ¼-inch eggplant pulp in the shells when you hollow them out. If you're not a fan of eggplant, substitute zucchini; just remember that it will cook a little more quickly.

Total time: 41 minutes

  2 eggplants, cut in half lengthwise (about 3 pounds)
  ¼ cup water
     Cooking spray
  1 cup chopped onion
  1 cup chopped plum tomato
  ¼ cup white wine
  3 garlic cloves, minced
  1 cup (4 ounces) crumbled feta cheese
  ½ cup chopped fresh parsley, divided
  ¾ teaspoon salt, divided
  ¼ teaspoon freshly ground black pepper
  2 (1-ounce) slices French bread
  2 tablespoons grated fresh Parmesan cheese

1. Carefully remove pulp from each eggplant, reserving shells. Coarsely chop pulp to measure 6 cups. Place eggplant shells, cut sides down, in a 10-inch square baking dish. Add ¼ cup water to dish. Cover and microwave at HIGH 5 minutes or until shells are tender. Keep warm.

2. Preheat broiler.

3. Heat a large nonstick skillet over medium-high heat. Coat pan with cooking spray. Add eggplant pulp, and sauté 7 minutes. Add onion; sauté 2 minutes. Stir in tomato, wine, and garlic; cook 3 minutes or until liquid almost evaporates, stirring occasionally. Remove from heat; add feta cheese, ¼ cup parsley, ½ teaspoon salt, and black pepper, stirring to combine. Spoon ¾ cup eggplant mixture into each eggplant shell.

4. Place bread slices in a food processor; pulse 10 times or until coarse crumbs measure 1 cup. Combine the breadcrumbs, ¼ cup parsley, ¼ teaspoon salt, and Parmesan, stirring well. Sprinkle ¼ cup breadcrumb mixture over each stuffed shell. Arrange shells on a baking sheet coated with cooking spray; broil 2 minutes or until lightly browned. Yield: 4 servings (serving size: 1 stuffed eggplant half).

CALORIES 250 (30% from fat); FAT 8.4g (sat 5.1g, mono 1.6g, poly 0.6g); PROTEIN 11.3g; CARB 35.3g; FIBER 10.3g; CHOL 29mg; IRON 2.3mg; SODIUM 906mg; CALC 246mg

Penne with Tomatoes, Olives, and Capers

This simple dish depends on fresh basil, garlic, and tomatoes to deliver big flavor. You can use almost any small pasta, such as macaroni, farfalle, rotelle, or tubetti.

Total time: 22 minutes

1 tablespoon olive oil
¼ teaspoon crushed red pepper
3 garlic cloves, finely chopped
3 cups chopped plum tomato (about 1¾ pounds)
½ cup chopped pitted kalamata olives
1½ tablespoons capers
¼ teaspoon salt
6 cups hot cooked penne (about 4 cups uncooked tube-shaped pasta)
¾ cup (3 ounces) grated fresh Parmesan cheese
3 tablespoons chopped fresh basil

1. Heat olive oil in a large nonstick skillet over medium-high heat. Add red pepper and chopped garlic, and sauté 30 seconds. Add tomato, olives, capers, and salt. Reduce heat, and simmer 8 minutes, stirring occasionally. Add pasta to pan, tossing gently to coat; cook 1 minute or until thoroughly heated. Remove from heat.

2. Spoon pasta mixture into a large bowl; top with cheese and basil, tossing gently. Yield: 4 servings (serving size: about 1¾ cups).

CALORIES 484 (28% from fat); FAT 15.1g (sat 4.7g, mono 7.7g, poly 1.7g); PROTEIN 19.1g; CARB 67.8g; FIBER 4.3g; CHOL 14mg; IRON 3.9mg; SODIUM 870mg; CALC 287mg

Quick Tip: You'll save time in the kitchen if you buy pitted olives.

Menu   SERVES 4

Penne with Tomatoes, Olives, and Capers

Parmesan bread twists
Combine ¼ cup grated fresh Parmesan cheese and ½ teaspoon black pepper. Unroll 1 (11-ounce) can refrigerated breadstick dough; cut dough along perforations to form 12 breadsticks. Sprinkle cheese mixture over dough, gently pressing into dough. Twist each breadstick, and place on a baking sheet coated with cooking spray. Bake at 375° for 13 minutes or until breadsticks are lightly browned.

Green salad

Game Plan

1 While oven heats and water comes to a boil:
• Prepare breadsticks
• Chop tomato, olives, and basil
• Grate cheese

2 While tomato mixture cooks:
• Cook pasta
• Toss salad

Sandwiches

Make sandwich night more than a meal
on the run with these inspiring menus.

Menu

Baked Cornmeal-Crusted Grouper Sandwich
with Tartar Sauce

Pickle spears

Baked potato chips

Pineapple-coconut sorbet with macadamia nuts
Stir 1 tablespoon cream of coconut (such as Coco Lopez) into 1 pint softened pineapple sorbet. Freeze to desired consistency. Spoon into dessert dishes; top each serving with 1 tablespoon toasted coconut and 1 teaspoon chopped macadamia nuts.

Game Plan

1 While oven heats:
- Bread fish fillets
- Soften sorbet

2 While fish cooks:
- Prepare tartar sauce
- Prepare sorbet

Quick Tip:

You can prepare the tartar sauce in advance; cover and refrigerate.

Baked Cornmeal-Crusted Grouper Sandwich with Tartar Sauce

Choose any mild fish that's locally available and in season; cod, halibut, and sole are good choices.

Total time: 35 minutes

TARTAR SAUCE:
- ½ cup low-fat mayonnaise
- 2 tablespoons chopped green onions
- 1 tablespoon sweet pickle relish
- 1½ teaspoons capers
- 1½ teaspoons lemon juice
- ½ teaspoon Worcestershire sauce

GROUPER:
- ½ cup yellow cornmeal
- ½ teaspoon salt
- ¼ teaspoon ground red pepper
- ¼ cup 2% reduced-fat milk
- 4 (6-ounce) grouper fillets
- Cooking spray

ADDITIONAL INGREDIENT:
- 4 (1½-ounce) hamburger buns, split

1. Preheat oven to 450°.

2. To prepare tartar sauce, combine mayonnaise and next 5 ingredients (through Worcestershire), stirring with a whisk.

3. To prepare grouper, combine cornmeal, salt, and pepper in a shallow dish, stirring well. Place milk in a shallow bowl.

4. Dip each fillet in milk; dredge in cornmeal mixture. Place fish on a baking sheet coated with cooking spray. Bake at 450° for 10 minutes or until fish is done, turning once.

5. Spread about 2 tablespoons tartar sauce over cut sides of each bun; place 1 fish fillet on bottom half of each bun. Top fillets with the remaining bun halves. Yield: 4 servings.

CALORIES 443 (29% from fat); FAT 14.3g (sat 2.6g, mono 4.5g, poly 6.6g); PROTEIN 38.5g; CARB 38.3g; FIBER 2.5g; CHOL 75mg; IRON 3.2mg; SODIUM 961mg; CALC 110mg

Falafel-Stuffed Pitas

Grape and walnut salad

Combine ½ cup plain low-fat yogurt, 2 tablespoons brown sugar, and a dash of ground cinnamon in a medium bowl. Add 3 cups halved red seedless grapes and 3 tablespoons chopped walnuts; stir well to combine.

Iced mint tea

Game Plan

1 Prepare grape salad; cover and chill.

2 While falafel patties cook:
• Prepare sauce
• Slice tomato
• Wash lettuce
• Prepare tea

Quick Tip: To prevent the falafel mixture from sticking as you shape the patties, dip your hands in water before forming them.

Falafel-Stuffed Pitas

The patties will seem small when you're forming them, but they fit perfectly in the pita halves. Look for tahini (sesame-seed paste) near the peanut butter.

Total time: 30 minutes

FALAFEL PATTIES:
¼   cup dry breadcrumbs
¼   cup chopped fresh cilantro
1½ teaspoons ground cumin
½   teaspoon salt
¼   teaspoon ground red pepper
2   garlic cloves, crushed
1   large egg
1   (15-ounce) can chickpeas (garbanzo beans), drained
1   tablespoon olive oil

TAHINI SAUCE:
½   cup plain low-fat yogurt
2   tablespoons fresh lemon juice
2   tablespoons tahini
1   garlic clove, minced

REMAINING INGREDIENTS:
4   (6-inch) whole wheat pitas, cut in half
8   curly leaf lettuce leaves
16 (¼-inch-thick) slices tomato

1. To prepare falafel patties, place first 8 ingredients in a food processor, and process mixture until smooth. Divide mixture into 16 equal portions; shape each portion into a ¼-inch-thick patty. Heat oil in a large nonstick skillet over medium-high heat. Add patties; cook 5 minutes on each side or until patties are browned.

2. To prepare tahini sauce, combine low-fat yogurt, lemon juice, tahini, and 1 minced garlic clove in a small bowl, stirring mixture with a whisk. Spread about 1½ tablespoons tahini sauce into each pita half. Fill each pita half with 1 curly leaf lettuce leaf, 2 tomato slices, and 2 falafel patties. Yield: 4 servings (serving size: 2 stuffed pita halves).

CALORIES 403 (28% from fat); FAT 12.6g (sat 1.9g, mono 5.6g, poly 3.9g); PROTEIN 15g; CARB 59g; FIBER 6.8g; CHOL 56mg; IRON 4.4mg; SODIUM 901mg; CALC 188mg

Shrimp Po'boy with Spicy Ketchup

A New Orleans specialty, this sandwich is often made with deep-fried shrimp. Oven-frying the shrimp, which are coated in garlicky breadcrumbs, delivers big flavor without the fat.

Total time: 34 minutes

- 3 tablespoons dry breadcrumbs
- ¼ teaspoon salt
- ¼ teaspoon black pepper
- 1 garlic clove, minced
- 1 tablespoon olive oil
- 1 pound large shrimp, peeled and deveined
- ¼ cup ketchup
- 1½ teaspoons fresh lemon juice
- ½ teaspoon Worcestershire sauce
- ¼ teaspoon chili powder
- ¼ teaspoon hot sauce
- 2 (10-inch) submarine rolls, split
- 2 cups torn curly leaf lettuce
- ½ cup thinly sliced red onion

1. Prepare broiler.

2. Line a baking sheet with heavy-duty aluminum foil. Combine first 4 ingredients in a medium bowl, stirring with a fork. Combine oil and shrimp; toss well. Place half of the shrimp in breadcrumb mixture; toss well to coat. Place breaded shrimp in a single layer on prepared baking sheet. Repeat procedure with the remaining shrimp and breadcrumb mixture. Broil 4 minutes or until shrimp are done.

3. Combine ketchup, juice, Worcestershire, chili powder, and hot sauce in a small bowl, stirring with a whisk.

4. Spread 2 tablespoons ketchup mixture over cut sides of each roll half. Place 1 cup lettuce over bottom half of each roll, and top with ¼ cup onion. Arrange 1 cup shrimp on each roll half; top with remaining roll half. Cut sandwiches in half. Yield: 4 servings (serving size: 1 sandwich half).

CALORIES 401 (20% from fat); FAT 9.1g (sat 1.7g, mono 4.6g, poly 1.7g); PROTEIN 30g; CARB 48.9g; FIBER 3g; CHOL 172mg; IRON 5.3mg; SODIUM 864mg; CALC 183mg

Quick Tip: Substitute vacuum-packed whole kernel corn for fresh to save time.

Menu   SERVES 4

Shrimp Po'boy with
Spicy Ketchup

Corn salad

Heat a nonstick skillet over medium heat. Add 2 cups fresh corn kernels, and cook 5 minutes, stirring frequently. Combine corn, ½ cup chopped red bell pepper, 2 tablespoons chopped fresh parsley, 2 tablespoons chopped red onion, 1½ tablespoons fresh lime juice, 1 teaspoon olive oil, ¼ teaspoon salt, and ⅛ teaspoon black pepper, tossing gently.

Fresh strawberries

Game Plan

1 Prepare corn salad.

2 While broiler heats:
- Prepare breadcrumb mixture
- Toss shrimp in oil
- Coat shrimp in breadcrumb mixture

3 While shrimp cooks:
- Prepare ketchup mixture
- Slice rolls
- Tear lettuce and slice onion
- Wash and halve strawberries

Menu SERVES 4

Salad Niçoise in Pita Pockets

Potato salad

Combine 2 tablespoons fresh lemon juice, 2 tablespoons light mayonnaise, 2 tablespoons fat-free sour cream, ½ teaspoon salt, and ¼ teaspoon pepper in a large bowl, stirring with a whisk. Add 2 pounds cooked quartered small red potato, ½ cup chopped green onions, and 2 strips of bacon, cooked and crumbled; stir to combine.

Lemonade

Game Plan

1 While potato cooks:
- Chop green onions
- Cook bacon
- Combine mayonnaise mixture
- Pit and chop olives

2 While green beans cool:
- Combine tuna, olives, and capers
- Prepare dressing

Salad Niçoise in Pita Pockets

Fresh green beans give this tuna sandwich, inspired by the classic Mediterranean salad, an interesting crunch. Cooking the beans in the microwave saves time.

Total time: 30 minutes

- 1 cup (1-inch) cut fresh green beans (about 4 ounces)
- 1 tablespoon water
- ¼ cup niçoise olives, pitted and chopped (about 18 olives)
- 1 tablespoon capers
- 1 (12-ounce) can solid white tuna in water, drained
- 1 tablespoon extravirgin olive oil
- 1 tablespoon fresh lemon juice
- ½ teaspoon salt
- 2 (6-inch) whole wheat pitas, cut in half
- 4 curly leaf lettuce leaves

1. Combine beans and water in a small microwave-safe bowl; cover. Microwave at HIGH 1½ minutes or until beans are crisp-tender; drain. Rinse with cold water. Drain; cool. Combine beans, olives, capers, and tuna.

2. Combine oil, juice, and salt, stirring with a whisk. Pour oil mixture over tuna mixture; toss gently to coat.

3. Line each pita half with 1 lettuce leaf; spoon about ½ cup tuna mixture into each pita half. Yield: 4 servings (serving size: 1 stuffed pita half).

CALORIES 253 (30% from fat); FAT 8.3g (sat 1.5g, mono 4.4g, poly 1.7g); PROTEIN 24.1g; CARB 21.6g; FIBER 4.2g; CHOL 36mg; IRON 2.6mg; SODIUM 702mg; CALC 48mg

Quick Tip: If you're short on time, use frozen quartered red potatoes.

Smoky Bacon and Blue Cheese Chicken Salad Pitas

This tangy sandwich filling will remind you of the classic BLT. You can make the chicken salad ahead, and place it in pita halves just before serving.

Total time: 20 minutes

¾   cup plain fat-free yogurt
¼   cup (1 ounce) crumbled blue cheese
2   tablespoons light mayonnaise
½   teaspoon freshly ground black pepper
3   cups shredded romaine lettuce
1½ cups shredded cooked chicken (about 6 ounces)
4   bacon slices, cooked and crumbled
2   medium tomatoes, seeded and chopped

4   (6-inch) whole wheat pitas, cut in half

1. Combine first 4 ingredients, stirring well. Combine lettuce, chicken, bacon, and tomatoes in a medium bowl, stirring well. Drizzle the yogurt mixture over chicken mixture; toss gently to coat. Spoon ½ cup chicken salad into each pita half. Serve immediately. Yield: 4 servings (serving size: 2 stuffed pita halves).

CALORIES 375 (29% from fat); FAT 12.1g (sat 3.7g, mono 3.6g, poly 3.1g); PROTEIN 26.1g; CARB 43.8g; FIBER 6.3g; CHOL 55mg; IRON 3.5mg; SODIUM 696mg; CALC 130mg

Quick Tip: To save time and avoid peeling and cutting whole carrots, use three cups of bagged baby carrots.

Menu   SERVES 4

Smoky Bacon and Blue Cheese Chicken Salad Pitas

Herbed carrots

Cook 3 cups (1½-inch) pieces peeled carrots in boiling water for 5 minutes or until crisp-tender. Drain well. Rinse with cold water; drain. Combine 3 tablespoons white wine vinegar, 1 tablespoon extra-virgin olive oil, 1 teaspoon dried oregano, 1 teaspoon salt, ½ teaspoon freshly ground black pepper, and 1 minced garlic clove; drizzle over carrots. Cover and chill until ready to serve.

Fresh berries

Game Plan

1 Prepare carrots; cover and chill.

2 While carrots chill:
  • Prepare salad
  • Place salad in pita halves

Menu

SERVES 4

Gyros

Greek salad

Combine 2 teaspoons olive oil, 1 teaspoon fresh lemon juice, ½ teaspoon salt, and ¼ teaspoon freshly ground black pepper, stirring well with a whisk. Combine 6 cups mixed salad greens, 2 cups chopped tomato, and ¼ cup (1 ounce) crumbled feta cheese in a large bowl. Add oil mixture; toss gently to coat. Serve immediately.

Vanilla yogurt with honey

Game Plan

1 While broiler heats:
- Prepare meat mixture
- Drain cucumber and onion for sauce

2 While meat cooks:
- Prepare sauce for gyros
- Prepare salad

Quick Tip: Lemon juice is used in the meat mixture, sauce, and salad, so squeeze enough for all at one time.

Gyros

A Greek specialty, gyros are traditionally made from spiced, spit-roasted lamb. In this recipe, we mold a ground lamb mixture into loaves. The yogurt-cucumber sauce is a variation on another traditional Greek favorite, tzatziki.

Total time: 19 minutes

LOAVES:
- 1 teaspoon onion powder
- 1 teaspoon garlic powder
- 1 teaspoon dried oregano
- 2 teaspoons fresh lemon juice
- ¼ teaspoon salt
- 3 garlic cloves, minced
- 6 ounces ground lamb
- 6 ounces ground sirloin
- Cooking spray
- ⅛ teaspoon ground red pepper

SAUCE:
- 1 cup peeled shredded cucumber
- ¼ cup vertically sliced red onion
- 1 tablespoon chopped fresh mint
- ½ teaspoon garlic powder
- ½ teaspoon fresh lemon juice
- ⅛ teaspoon salt
- ⅛ teaspoon black pepper
- 1 (8-ounce) carton plain fat-free yogurt

REMAINING INGREDIENT:
- 4 pocketless pitas

1. Preheat broiler.

2. To prepare loaves, combine first 8 ingredients. Divide mixture in half, forming each half into a 6 x 3–inch loaf. Place each loaf on a broiler pan coated with cooking spray; broil for 7 minutes on each side or until done.

3. Sprinkle loaves with ground red pepper. Cut each loaf crosswise into (⅛-inch) slices.

4. To prepare sauce, place cucumber and red onion onto several layers of heavy-duty paper towels. Cover with additional paper towels, and let stand 5 minutes.

5. Combine cucumber mixture, mint, and the next 5 ingredients (through yogurt), stirring well. Divide meat slices among pitas; top each serving with about ¼ cup sauce. Yield: 4 servings (serving size: 1 sandwich).

CALORIES 375 (28% from fat); FAT 11.6g (sat 4.4g, mono 4.7g, poly 1g); PROTEIN 25g; CARB 42.4g; FIBER 2.3g; CHOL 61mg; IRON 3.5mg; SODIUM 627mg; CALC 158mg

how to use it and why

Glance at the end of any *Cooking Light* recipe, and you'll see how committed we are to helping you make the best of today's light cooking. With six chefs, three registered dietitians, five home economists, and a computer system that analyzes every ingredient we use, *Cooking Light* gives you authoritative dietary detail that you won't find in any other epicurean magazine.

We go to great lengths to show you how our recipes fit into your healthful eating plan. If you're trying to lose weight, the calorie and fat figures probably will help most. But if you're keeping a close eye on the sodium, cholesterol, and saturated fat in your diet, we provide those numbers, too. And because many women don't get enough iron or calcium, we can help you there. Finally, there's a fiber analysis to help you make sure that you get enough roughage.

what it means and how we get there

Besides the calories, protein, fat, fiber, iron, and sodium we list at the end of each recipe, there are a few things we abbreviate for space.

- *sat* for saturated fat
- *CARB* for carbohydrates
- *g* for gram
- *mono* for monounsaturated fat
- *CHOL* for cholesterol
- *mg* for milligram
- *poly* for polyunsaturated fat
- *CALC* for calcium

We get numbers for those categories based on a few assumptions:

- When we give a range for an ingredient (3 to 3½ cups flour, for instance), we calculate the lesser amount.
- Some alcohol calories evaporate during heating; we reflect that.
- Only the amount of marinade absorbed by the food is calculated.

your daily nutrition guide

	women ages 25 to 50	women over 50	men over 24
Calories	2,000	2,000 or less	2,700
Protein	50g	50g or less	63g
Fat	65g or less	65g or less	88g or less
Saturated Fat	20g or less	20g or less	27g or less
Carbohydrates	304g	304g	410g
Fiber	25g to 35g	25g to 35g	25g to 35g
Cholesterol	300mg or less	300mg or less	300mg or less
Iron	18mg	8mg	8mg
Sodium	2,300mg or less	1,500mg or less	2,300mg or less
Calcium	1,000mg	1,200mg	1,000mg

Calorie requirements vary according to your size, weight, and level of activity. This chart is a good general guide; additional nutrients are needed during some stages of life. For example, kids' calorie and protein needs are based on height and vary greatly as they grow. Teenagers require less protein but more calcium and slightly more iron than adults. Pregnant or breast-feeding women need more protein, calories, and calcium. The need for iron increases during pregnancy but returns to normal after birth.

The nutritional values used in our calculations either come from a computer program produced by Computrition Inc., The Food Processor, Version 7.5 (ESHA Research), or are provided by food manufacturers.

recipe index

A reference for all 81 entrées in this book

61

83